When Angels Speak

22 Angel Communicators Connect You To The Guidance Of The Angels

Compiled by Kyra Schaefer

As You Wish Publishing, LLC Kyra@asyouwishpublishing.com
602-592-1141

ISBN-13: 978-1-7324982-9-7

ISBN-10: 1-7324982-9-6

Compiled by Kyra Schaefer

Edited by Todd Schaefer and Karen Oschmann

Cover Design by Todd Schaefer

Printed in the United States of America.

Nothing in this book or any affiliations with this book is a substitute for medical or psychological help. If you are needing help please seek it.

Dedication

To The Angels

TABLE OF CONTENTS

Foreword
by Kyra Schaefer

Are angels real? I have often wondered how much of the angelic interactions I have experienced were real versus imagined. Perhaps, you have asked yourself a similar question. Are angels real, and if they are, how do I connect with them? In the following pages, your angel communicators will strive to connect you with the wisdom of the angelic realm. But before you go, let's talk about what angels are and what they are not.

Angels Are:

Angels are believed to be our helpers and gifts from God. They have been a prevalent part of our ancient human history. Plato and Aristotle both believed in angels and their effect on human consciousness. "Angels" (derived from the Hebrew word "anglos," meaning "messenger") are thought to be beings bathed in white light with a hardwired connection to God. Or if you prefer a different nomenclature: source, universe or all that is.

They are here to protect, guide, and love us on our soul journey toward enlightenment. They are unconditional love and want only for our happiness. They are believed to be present anytime we call upon their help, and they may or may not be in a position to answer our call. They will deliver messages we want to hear and don't want to hear. I had an encounter with an angel who affectionately asked me to suck it up. She knew I was sabotaging myself, and without that gritty wisdom, I wouldn't have been able to move forward.

Angels Are Not:

Angels are not wish-granting machines. Just because you want something doesn't mean it is their job to deliver it. They won't always tell you what you want to hear. I often ask my angels, "Why all of this chaos? Why all the pain and suffering? Why are there people in power who can make a difference but choose not to? Why are we here?" The answer is consistent: "This is for the development of the soul, not for the protection of the body." I'm so daft I have to ask the same question over and over again, especially when I feel discouraged. My human mind often doesn't like the answer, although my heart knows it is accurate.

Communicating With Angels:

Your angels are always communicating; however, you may not be in a position to interpret their message without some education. If you are wondering how to strengthen your connection to the angelic realm, you are in the right place. In the following chapters, you will learn just that.

Learning how to connect with your angels is a very slippery slope. We can fall into the trap of confusing our ego with an angelic message. Our ego can put us down, but it will also find other ways to sabotage us with false confidence or lack of humility. Learning to tell the difference is crucial.

During a conflict, an angelic message will always offer the person you are in conflict with their innocence. They will fight on the side of unconditional love and for your integrity. In essence, they always assume positive intent because that is the truth in all things. We are all innocent and everything is for our good, even if it feels bad at the time.

FOREWORD

In the following chapters, you will be able to learn from the experts how to genuinely connect to your Archangels, guardian angels, earth angels, and the angelic realm. Through these connections, you will draw yourself closer to the unconditional love of the angels in a variety of ways. Your angels are here to love you through the highs and lows of this lifetime. Allow that peace to permeate all your worries and concerns. You are never alone.

Kyra Schaefer, founder of As You Wish Publishing, is dedicated to helping authors avoid rejection and getting their message heard. You can learn about upcoming projects you can contribute to at www.asyouwishpublishing.com.

CHAPTER

Teachings Of My Son
By Anne Danielle Gingras

ANNE DANIELLE GINGRAS

Anne Gingras embraces life. She is a wife, a mother, a sister, a daughter, a teacher, an author, and a friend. She holds an Honors Bachelor in Arts (Music) from the University of Ottawa, a B.Ed from Laurentian University, and an Honorary Doctorate of Education (honoris causa) from Nipissing University. She completed a doctoral diploma in Applied Metaphysics. As a Holding Space practitioner, Anne is an advocate for promoting emotional connections, and often involves clients in projects which will impact their learning and serve as a basis to actions geared towards reaching their life purpose. She is also the author of the book, *The Old Man on the Bench*. In her spare moments, Anne enjoys composing music, writing, traveling, and meeting with clients to offer her intuitive insights. She can be reached at annegingras@me.com or on her Facebook page: Anne Gingras—Postcards from the Soul.

Acknowledgments

Thank you to my soul families, both on earth and the astral planes. You are my anchors. You help me soar and dream so that I can create the incredible journey in which I have the privilege to grow daily. Everlasting love and respect to the man who chose to share his life with our children and me; I will love you forever. You are a shining presence in my life. I send immense gratitude to my twin flame who still holds my heart and soul after countless lives and adventures together. I have loved you always—and you are 'stuck' with me. You are brave. To the wolf, my spirit animal who protects and defends me in all realms, keep leading the pack.

Teachings Of My Son
By Anne Danielle Gingras

It came at me like the sound of felted footsteps in the night.

I married when I was 22 years old. Some would argue that I was too young at the time and that I hadn't had a chance to grow up. I understand now that had I waited longer, I would never have had the opportunity to experience motherhood. I am a woman with autism—and statistics show that we are more apt to live alone, with our dreams and ambitions. The Universe had other plans. But let's start this tale at the beginning.

In 1993, we became parents to a beautiful baby boy. We named him Alex. I cried as I held him for the first time. I had no life experience. This was new, but I dove in. I loved Alex with all of my heart. I held him for hours, smelled him, smiled at him, and watched him sleep. When he was awake, Alex held my gaze and tried to fit his fist into his mouth. He had peculiar likes and dislikes, but I never paid much attention to them. He grew, and all seemed typical—until his first birthday. Society dictated that a cake be made and that we put his hands in the cake. He'd cry, we'd take pictures and smile—a great memory. A chocolate cake was set before him, and we encouraged him to touch it. He refused, clearly agitated. My mother-in-law stuck his hands in the cake, and that was it. Alex shrieked and had the biggest tantrum. People laughed. My heart broke because it was on that day that I felt things were going to be forever different for him. Soon after, we bathed him and calmed him down. He eventually smiled, swaddled in his little soft Winnie the

Pooh pajamas. He fell asleep on me that evening, and I vowed never to let go of him. He was different. I just didn't know why. There is something to be said about the innocence of embarking on a life-long project. Often, we see the scope of things beforehand.

At eighteen months, Alex had minimal language and unusual behaviors: words fascinated him, and he ate the same foods. When driving somewhere, he threw tantrums if we changed direction. He refused to have his hair washed, and cringed when he touched slimy food. He barely slept, so we watched him, afraid that he would run away because he had figured out latches and clasps on doors. Alex would frequently bang his head on the floor for seconds, minutes, and usually hours. When we brought him to the hospital, they wondered if we were abusive. Many passed comments. We were ignored and judged. We were, after all, only young parents—*new* parents—and everybody offered advice. I felt alone, angry, and terrified of what the future held for us. I was failing when my son was not even two years old; I didn't want a part of this anymore. In my head, I had packed my suitcase and moved on. I felt that I was stuck, unable to offer Alex the best learning opportunities. I dreaded the unexpected. The Universe had started whispering wisdom through dreams while I slept, but I never took the time to pay attention to the messages. Life was all about getting up, eating, taking care of Alex, and going back to sleep. Press repeat the next morning and do it all over again. I didn't smile. I felt that, except for my husband, there was no one around to help.

Fast Forward: The distant memories are still raw. When he was four and a half years old, on a fated afternoon and on the verge of losing all the services we had obtained for him, Alex received the diagnosis of autism. The pediatrician told us that he would never go to regular school, and would be placed in an institution. He looked at his watch, wished us well, and sent us on our way. The real challenges were only beginning. We had no idea where to turn for help; it was as though the Universe had handed us a life sentence, while, in essence, it had given us the best gift it could have. We finally had a word for what was going on. We didn't know what to do, but it was a start. Would he ever talk? What would happen to him? To us?

Flashback: I am three years old. The phone rings, and I tell my mother who it is before she answers. There is no call display at that time. I am right. Multiply this occurrence a hundred times.

Flashback: A young girl goes to sleep and dreams. When she awakens, she remembers details about people and places. Later on, that day or that week, things come to pass. Multiply this occurrence hundreds of times.

Flashback: A teenager enters a room full of people and looks around at them. She sees the energy and senses emotions. She has to leave because it becomes too intense to stay around so many individuals. Multiply this occurrence hundreds of times.

Flashback: The twenty-nine-year-old mother of a beautiful young child is sitting in her office late at night. She looks up and comes face-to-face with the reflection of her grandmother. The migraines that she has been plagued with for months instantly lift, and she can sense and know things.

Multiply this occurrence hundreds, perhaps even thousands of times.

These flashbacks marked the beginning of my spiritual adventure. I had always been able to know what others couldn't. I was an empath, I felt too much, I knew too much—and I was about to rediscover these abilities.

When I turned 33, we moved to my parents' house. It was time for a change. Alex was growing up and in school full-time. We wanted to leave behind the memories—tantrums, battles for services, never-ending repetition of routines. It was the moment to embrace change and to move on. We now had two children, and life was advancing. Often, I would pray for a miracle. I also cursed the Universe for giving us the responsibility of raising someone with autism. I was weak and wanted no part of it. I would sit for long periods and fixate—wondering what I could do or what I had done so wrong to have to be experiencing such hardship. How unfair that my beautiful son had to fight so hard every day. Speech was difficult for him. He had no friends because he lacked social skills, and sensory input drove him insane. How would we ever be able to help him? The world was a cruel place to live in. Society dictated parameters, and he fit none of them.

The answer came one afternoon when I was sitting in my living room with Alex. He was on the couch, playing with his toys. I can't recall which little figurines were enticing him at the moment, but I do remember that it was a sunny afternoon. Alex was chattering away when suddenly, he stopped playing. He looked at me—and transformed. Into the body of the young, seven-year-old child entered energy, which I had never encountered. His eyes changed, and Alex began speaking extremely clearly, in an unrecognizable voice. It was a deep, calm voice which was articulate and sounded as though it were from another realm. I heard, "Anne, I chose to have autism so that I can teach others around me how to be gentle and loving. You cannot and will never be able to "cure" me, as that is not my chosen path. Trust in who you are and in what you can do. Let me make decisions, and let others learn by my mistakes. I am here to change the world—to change *your* world—and you must allow me to do so. I am well. I am okay. I have chosen you to be my parents. Guide me—advocate for me and for others—but do not ever doubt for one moment that this can be changed, for it will never be. I am here to change people's hearts—one person's heart at a time—and I will do so by encountering many individuals in my lifetime. Allow me to do so. Help me do so. Together, we will change the world." As suddenly as "he" had come, the higher being was gone. Alex looked up, giggled, and began playing again. I sat, bewildered by what I had witnessed. I cried. No one would ever believe such a thing; I was likely exhausted. That night, I told my husband what had happened, and he bawled. He too knew that we were not alone, and that our son would indeed change the world. We hugged each other and agreed to watch as life would evolve us. We still have no explanation of what transpired.

Life continued, and I never forgot the words of Alex when his higher self spoke to us. I couldn't remain unmarked by such declarations. Everything shifted at that moment. I changed my mindset and advocated for Alex—for him to evolve and pursue his mission of changing people's hearts. Things did not transform overnight for him.

Institutions wanted matters to look right, but when we observed what was occurring, it was apparent that specific individuals were pretending to help us as a family, and that they believed that Alex would never accomplish much. I like to think that many of those on our path were doing the best that they could, at the moment, with what little they understood of autism. Since I had heard the higher being, I trusted more in the outcomes than I had ever done in the past. I kept pushing the boundaries of regulations, accepting and advocating for what was allowed, and thus, obtained the best services for our son to progress to his full potential. What changed that day is the way that I now *saw* my son. I believed that he had chosen us to be his host family, and that he would be teaching higher lessons of tolerance and love to individuals on his path. It is what he had set out to do.

Everywhere Alex went, he touched hearts. He reached teachers and administration. When told that he would never graduate, Alex proved everyone wrong. He displayed both dedication and commitment. Now a well-spoken, young gentleman, he had developed numerous friendships with individuals. He touched lives and melted hearts with his words and his kind-hearted nature. He never spoke ill of anybody, and when things became difficult, he never engaged in conflict with anybody. Alex was teaching me how to become a tolerant, well-spoken adult, and how to spread light around me. I was learning about the importance of empathy and self-discipline, and how crucial it was to remain calm in moments when a single word can destroy relationships. I understood that connections were what mattered in life, and how incredibly important it was to be thankful for small moments. As a teacher, I had believed that curriculum and performance mattered. I changed my whole philosophy when I realized how wrong I had been. People would remember me for how I taught them. I witnessed my son evolve every day, and became a softer, more loving, and caring human being. Life brought forth other lessons, and I believe that because of everything that I was experiencing because of Alex, I had become ready to take them on.

The empathy skills I perfected helped me endure the devastating, life-altering decision I took when we placed my mother in a nursing care facility because of her dementia. As I cried, Alex kissed me on the cheek, reminding me that he loved me. In the same breath, he inquired about the meal plans, thus grounding me back to where I needed to be— here, in the moment, instead of flying away with my worrisome thoughts. Though frustrated, I was transforming into a gentler person, observing moments, and letting them go if they did not serve our healing purpose. I still got agitated when injustices were served, or when people told me to be reasonable. But I was also becoming tolerant, as he was, of people who also struggled. It is because of his presence in my life that I realized that everybody we met on our journey had a story, their individual life-map, and that it wasn't always easy for them either.

When Alex's path took him to college, I smiled proudly. He was a far step away from where he had been years ago, and he wanted to try his hand out at higher education. (I smile as I write this because he *is* the higher being). He did well in the academic portions, yet after not succeeding in the social requirements to be with young children, he decided, with my husband by his side, to move on to his other path—and dropped out of college. Our son stood up and took his place in the world. He had not failed, he had arrived. We were still his caretakers, but he was taking care of his and our destinies.

Alex's journey has taken him in a whole other direction. After joining Community Living, the incredible organization which supports his lifestyle challenges, he became a full-time employee at our local literacy alliance. Every day, he meets adults and helps them start a new path. He never judges, and is always patient with every person he meets. His words encourage, calm, and direct those who need reassurance. To him, there is no other way to be. "Never give up," he tells us, and them, as he moves calmly through his day and routines. I have learned a lot of lessons from my son. The most important one is that everyone can learn, in their individual way, and in their individual time. There are always options, and deadlines are never imperative.

When life becomes challenging, Alex still reminds me that laughing is the best antidote. I often hear him giggling uncontrollably as he watches videos or shares memes on social media. This twenty-six-year-old man has the soul of a sage and the heart of an innocent child. He can discuss the philosophy of doctoral graduates and play with figurines with a five-year-old child. He doesn't discern between the rich or the poor, the races or the abilities. In his eyes, we are one—humans with heart and a mission to make the world better. He does this only by *being*, every day, armed with love as his weapon and with the world as his canvas. To be his mother, his friend, and his caretaker has been the most humbling adventure of my human life—and I cannot wait to see where the future takes us.

CHAPTER

Two

Follow Your Heart
By Catherine Anderson

CATHERINE ANDERSON

Catherine Anderson is an Angel Intuitive and holds a Master Angel Certification. Her career in cardiac ultrasound and diagnostics ignited a passion for working with individuals through Intuitive Heart readings. Together with God and her angels, Catherine shares information that inspires and opens space for healing, enabling people to move toward their highest potential. Catherine and her husband own and operate Follow Your Heart, a boutique in Sedona, Arizona. Their custom-designed jewelry store is filled with high angelic energy and showcases handpicked crystals from all

over the world. Many times Catherine is inspired to charge crystals with customer's intentions, often powerful messages come across for the individual. You may visit Catherine at the shop or schedule a phone reading by contacting her at sedonashore@gmail.com or
sedonaheartconnection.com

Acknowledgments

To Laura Rudacille, thank you for being my guiding light. Your encouragement and support helped make my chapter a reality. A special thanks to my husband Greg, who has always been and continues to be my biggest fan. My loving daughter Christina, your strength, focus, and determination continue to inspire me. Last but not least my mother, for your endless love and courage to let me fly when you needed me the most.

Follow Your Heart
By Catherine Anderson

My experience with clairvoyance began at an early age. As a little girl, I had spontaneous visions of people and strange places. My inability to control my reality terrified me. It was during these times that I began to see tall, beautiful angels who appeared with a loving and calming presence. I did not develop a deep personal relationship with them until later in life.

For many of us, personal crisis can initiate change. Mine began with a divorce after twenty-one years of marriage. Married at an early age, we were known as the perfect couple. As years passed, we had a beautiful daughter and built our dream home. By everyone's standards, we were living the perfect life. Like a tsunami, in one moment everything changed forever. I was completely devastated. I realized, to my horror, that I had no idea who I was. Somewhere in those twenty-one years, I had lost myself. I was terrified. I had no idea how to pick up the shattered pieces of my life. My heart guided me to go within. I began with prayer and meditation.

After my divorce was finalized, I drove out of town. I had to get out, to escape the chaos that was now my life. I yearned for a sign that everything would be alright. I got a hotel room along the beach. My first morning of becoming newly single, I sat naked on the floor in meditation and prayer facing the ocean as the sun was beginning to rise. I was stripped physically, mentally, and spiritually. My

16

nakedness was raw, real, and I was exposed in every sense of the word. With tears streaming down my face and with my broken heart, I spontaneously gave my life back to God. I asked Him to guide me to be of service to others. At that moment, the sun's rays raced across the ocean and hit my heart with an intense brilliance, and I was instantly bathed in a golden light taking my breath away. I felt immense peace and love, and I knew in that moment, it was a promise from God. He would be my light, and angels would be my guides.

I was compelled to roll up my sleeves and get busy doing an autopsy on myself and the past twenty-one years. I worked to create a new home, a sacred space where I could do my inner work. I was on a mission to discover who I was. I journaled my innermost pain. I cried an ocean of tears. I spent countless years in therapy and self-reflection. I discovered I was using my body as an emotional dumping ground for all my negative feelings. By stuffing and rejecting my unwanted emotions, I was unwittingly numbing myself to all my emotions. Once I started to peel back the thick layers of unacknowledged feelings, I began to feel on a deeper, more palpable level. I developed compassion, love, and respect for all aspects of myself.

My meditation and prayer practice was critical for my spiritual and personal growth. Being consistent each day, I began to experience moments of peace and calm. The more I focused, the more peaceful my mind and body felt. It was in those moments of peace that my angels were able to connect with me. I made the connection that the gentle, positive messages coming from my heart were angelic. Angels connect and communicate through the most powerful, intelligent organ in the body—the heart.

Over time my connection with angels strengthened. I began to feel and recognize angelic presence by their high, clear vibration. The more I acknowledged their presence, the more information I received. Every time I asked my angels for guidance, I received it. Help came in different ways— synchronistic events, an unexpected message from an unusual source, billboards, family, or friends. I learned that angelic messages are always positive and uplifting, never harsh or judgmental.

My spiritual life began to flourish. I started to meet like-minded people. I traveled to Sedona, Arizona. I quickly fell in love with the land and returned many times. One particular vacation was planned with a friend, who unexpectedly canceled. I decided I was going to cancel my trip as well, but my angels had other plans for me. While having dinner in a restaurant, a Tibetan monk gave me a message that I was meant to go to Sedona alone. I was surprised to meet a monk in Delaware, let alone that he would share a message with me. My flight was less than two weeks away; I had no plans, no reservations, only the message that I was to go alone. Little did I know that this decision would completely change the direction of my life.

The next day I sat down at my computer and asked my angels for guidance. Where am I to stay in Sedona? I was guided to two particular places—a bed and breakfast called The Dreammaker, and Angel Valley. The irony of the names was not lost to me. Everything quickly fell into place, but the haste of my decision and having no other plans made me feel uncomfortable. I asked my angels for confirmation that I was on the right path. While on a walk one day, a large feather appeared, and I knew in my heart that it was from my angels.

I was so pleased with my physical confirmation. I reverently took the feather and placed it on the table so I could see it, to serve as a reminder. I soon discovered that my angels have a sense of humor. Feather manifestations continued in the most unlikely of places. I had so much fun collecting them, and by the end of the two weeks, I had a drawer full of feathers.

When I arrived at The Dreammaker in Sedona, I walked out onto the balcony, and a white feather was falling from the sky. I put out my hand as it gently landed in my palm. I felt the power of my angelic guidance, and I knew I was exactly where I was meant to be. The synchronicity of all the feathers, culminating to a white feather falling from the sky in Sedona, Arizona at the exact moment of my arrival, dazzled my mind and filled my heart with joy and gratitude. It humbled me to think God and my angels had organized it all for me. After that, the feather manifestations stopped. Message received—don't be afraid to ask for signs from the angels because they are always ready to assist us.

During an angel meditation, as I walked the land, I asked for any messages and guidance. Suddenly the air became charged, the path and trees began to shimmer with high energy. Angels appeared on both sides of the path. They radiated love and gratitude that encompassed and cradled me. The communication came across as a clear knowing, "You must let go of what you have, to receive what is to come."

I made the decision to move to Sedona. Having a Type-A personality, I went to work finding a job. I knew in my heart that a job was going to manifest, because, in my mind, I was going to be moving to Sedona within six months.

My life-long career was in cardiac ultrasound and diagnostics. A highly specialized field which uses crystals to evaluate heart function and detect abnormalities. I loved my job; it was extremely fulfilling working with hearts. I felt I was making a difference, and reading people's hearts was my passion.

Preparing to move, I sent out resumes and spent a lot of time planning. I needed to have my Plan A, and then a backup plan, just in case. I found comfort and safety in an organized life. But all the doors remained closed to me; nothing was falling into place. I knew I was being held back. I struggled and continued to push forward in spite of the resistance. This went on for several years. I couldn't fathom why my move was not flowing. Meanwhile, the job that I'd once loved and had a passion for had become cumbersome, frustrating, and eventually painful. I couldn't understand why the doors of opportunity didn't fly open for me. I assumed the gates of heaven would open, the angels would sing, and my job would appear. What was wrong? I was missing something. Slowly, I began to realize my transition had to be a leap of faith. I was to relocate without a job, and the reason why would be revealed to me later.

My angel's message continued to be the same; "You must let go of what you have, to receive what is to come." Yet I didn't comprehend the scope of the message. I had to let go of everything, which included my beliefs that I needed to move forward with a safety net and backup plans. Once I realized what I was doing to block myself and decided to let go and trust everything fell into place.

When I told my family and friends that I was moving across the country without a plan, understandably, I was met with resistance. To the logical mind, my decision appeared crazy. Nobody in their right mind leaves their home, career, good money, family, friends, and moves across the country alone, without a job or viable plan. Everybody knows that you have to have a job before you leave your current job. Questions were raised—who are you going to work for? What are you going to do there? Who do you know there? My mother, who had always been supportive of my decisions, said with fear in her eyes that it was ridiculous, and I should wait until I retire. Despite everyone's fears, worry, and doubts, including mine, I continued forward with my plans. My consistent response to everyone's questions was: "I am following my heart."

A lot people asked how I knew I was making the right move. I had a particular a-ha moment that gave me courage through my transition to Sedona. My beautiful furniture had recently been sold and removed, and all that was left was a mattress and box springs on my bedroom floor. The scene was shocking and terrifying. My heart began to race; my mind, and body filled with terror and paralyzing self-doubt. My mind was telling me the move was all was a huge mistake and I would never make it. I would be alone and barely knew anyone in Sedona. You can't go without a plan, and there is no support out there. My mind raced with all the logical reasons as to why this could never work and how dangerous it was.

At that moment, my angels reached out and guided me to follow my heart, and I suddenly realized what my mind was doing. Intuitively, I dropped my awareness from my head into my heart and felt the rightness of my decision. This technique strengthened my resolve and gave me the courage to move ahead, even when my head was telling me to keep what I have, and not to risk it.

I finally arrived in Sedona, Arizona, on October 31, 2011.

Six months later, my angels guided me to the man of my dreams. Greg, my husband of six years now, loves and honors me in ways I never thought possible. I am blessed with someone who loves me unconditionally. He has been there for me, even when everything was broken. I'm grateful for our relationship, and he continues to rock my world with his endless compassion and understanding.

Together we created a successful shop called Follow Your Heart—a cleverly-disguised jewelry shop created with angelic assistance. We design jewelry and sell crystals, but our real mission is to encourage people to connect with their guidance through their hearts and angels. I continue to work with people's hearts, but in other ways. I do Intuitive Heart sessions, giving messages and information that inspire and empower individuals for personal growth.

I see clearly why I needed to quit my job and move with nothing in place. I didn't know this journey would be a beacon of light for others. I meet many people who come to Sedona looking for a mystical experience that will direct them from a life that is no longer working. I'm able to share my personal journey and be an example. When you follow your heart, your life will unfold in ways you can never imagine.

I could never have dreamed of this life when I was lost and broken. When I truly let go and let God and my angels guide me, miracles happened. Had I decided to wait until I had a job, I would still be in Delaware waiting.

As I sit here looking out my window at the majestic red rocks of Sedona, highlighting a brilliant blue sky, I am filled with a deep sense of appreciation. God and my angels guided me to a life beyond my dreams. I am thankful I had the courage to risk it all and to believe. With determination, focus, and a dash of grit, I created a better life for myself with the help of God and my angels.

Our minds hold us back in fear and doubt. Have the courage to go within and listen to your heart. Take time to disconnect from the outside world and reconnect with your heart. The mind thinks, but the heart knows. What are your angels whispering for you to do? In what way are you being nudged to take your next step?

The desires of our hearts are beacons of light, guiding us to our highest potential. Allow the angels to assist you by listening with your heart. I am proof that when angels speak, they to lead us to the life of our dreams.

CHAPTER

Three

Angels At Play
By Cathy Stuart

CATHY STUART

Cathy Stuart is a Certified Spiritual Counselor, Reiki Master Teacher, and Life Coach. Cathy does angel readings, personal coaching, spiritual mediumship, chakra balancing, and Reiki. Cathy is an ordained minister with the Madonna Interfaith. By following her intuition and her vast knowledge of what most would call "life experience," Cathy has been assisting her clients for over 20 years in releasing emotions and patterns. Her mission is to allow her clients to come to know through the practice and practicality of the art of mindfulness, who they are and why they have agreed to come into this lifetime; to assist clients in coming into a place of pure unconditional love of self through redirection of their energies that have prevented them, in this lifetime, from moving forward to a life of peace, love, and harmony. You can reach Cathy at 623-363-2746 and www.universalwisdom.com

Acknowledgments

I would like to acknowledge my husband, LeRoy, who understood and supported my gifts from the day we met. Your love and support always remind me to never give up on my work. To my mother and grandmother for their intuitive insights that have helped shape and design my life. I want to thank my sister Gayle who edits my work with love and listens with an open heart. To my sister Peggy, although you are in spirit with me, you are constantly reminding me of my spiritual path through your loving messages from the other side. Last, I would be remiss if I did not acknowledge with love the gifts from my angels, especially Catherine.

Angels At Play
By Cathy Stuart

At age seven, I encountered my first angel, Catherine. I was one of five children, and quiet time was not always possible. It was a warm day in Michigan, so I went outside and lay in the grass to think about this day. It was important to me to make sure that everything I did was okay. I was excited to take First Communion, but I also knew that the priest and the nuns were strict about how you walked down the aisle, and how you took the host, so I began to worry about messing up in front of everyone. I had closed my eyes from the sun, but suddenly, this bright light came through my eyelids. I opened my eyes to see what it could be, and the light came closer to me. I knew it was not the sun, as I could see the sun behind this bright light. It was as if this light had merged with my body. I heard a soft female voice telling me not to be afraid. I wasn't—I was mesmerized by the brilliance of this light. In Catechism class, I had been told that there is a guardian angel who watches over each of us, and I said a prayer to my angel every night. So, I wasn't afraid—I knew without a doubt that this was my guardian angel. I asked her if she had a name, and she told me that she did not, but if I wanted to give her one, I could. I chose to call her Catherine, as my name was Cathy and the nuns made fun of me and called me 'Just Cathy' because I did not have a proper saint's first name.

Catherine told me she was a messenger from God. She said that I had a mission in life, that I would need to trust my path and listen to the messages as I moved through it. She also said she would always be beside me and that I could call upon her any time I wanted. I told only my mother what I had seen and heard. My mother never scolded me or said I had dreamt this but told me to hold it quietly in my heart. I was giddy with this secret, and I would call upon Catherine as I moved through life. I learned through her how to work with my intuition and how to follow my path. Little did I know how big my path was and how many other angels would show up to help me.

Over the years, I learned how to hone my intuitive gifts. I knew I could *feel*, which is also known as an empathic or gut feeling. I could hear voices, sometimes in my head and sometimes outside of it as I had when I met Catherine. I could also get clarity when a song played on the radio, and I was able to know what to do next. I also learned that my strongest intuitive gift was inner "knowing." I didn't understand how I knew something without having read it in a book, seen it on TV, or heard it from anyone. I simply knew. That gift, over the years, was the hardest one to explain to anyone. I tell my students and my clients that it is as if you are standing in a library, a book falls on you, and you absorb the information. As I moved through life, I did not know that this path would lead me right to the threshold of opening Angel Wings in Scottsdale, Arizona, a beautiful store full of angels, fairies, books, music, jewelry, and amazing artists.

In April 1994, I began to receive signs that I was to open a store. I had never read an angel book until I was suddenly gifted with two books. An article out of the *Detroit Freepress* about an angel store arrived, and I saw a PBS special about Tara's Angels in California. The PBS special featured angel artist Andy Lakey, and I knew he was someone I needed to meet in person. All of this transpired over the course of one week. By October 1, 1994, on my 44th birthday, I opened Angel Wings in Kiva Courtyard in Scottsdale.

I called Andy Lakey, and told him I'd seen him on the show and that I had recently opened my angel store. After a near death experience, Andy saw seven angels that told him to paint 2000 angels. From 1990 to 2000 Andy painted, even though he had never painted before. I asked if he would be willing to come to Angel Wings and do an event with me. He was thrilled, and we set it up for February 1995. Andy's art hangs in the Vatican, as well as in many schools for the blind and is included in the art collections of many celebrities.

There were many incredible experiences with Andy and his work at Angel Wings. The one that comes to mind foremost happened the day before Thanksgiving. I had started to turn out the lights at Angel Wings, when I felt this intuitive pull to leave my doors open for a little while longer. It was already dark outside. I had turned on the outside spotlight and started to bring my eight-foot-tall angel, which was tied to the palm tree in front of the store, inside. When I felt the energy guiding me to stay open, I left my door open and went to the shop next door to tell my son that I would be another 30 minutes. I was gone for no more than a few minutes. When I returned to my store, I saw two women hugging each other and crying, and I saw a boy and a girl standing behind them. They were in front of two of Andy's angel paintings. I approached them and asked if they were okay. They said they had been walking down the street and saw my large angel, and it appeared as if the light was shining on her heads. They were both guided to come into the courtyard and check it out. I asked them if they knew each other and they said no, one was from Ohio and the other from Pennsylvania. Both of these women had lost a child on the same day four years earlier, hence my "seeing" the boy and girl. Both women had been searching for just the right angel to help with their grief. Each purchased an angel painting that day. Had it not been for that inner voice, that intuitive nudge, I would have closed my store earlier that day, as business had been very slow because of the Thanksgiving holiday, and these women would not have met and shared a very heartfelt moment in their grief.

I knew I had the ability to read people, to see their angels, guides, and loved ones who had crossed over. However, I was not ready to share this with the world—I was intimidated with the inner programming, "Who do you think you are?" It wasn't until 1998, when I attended a workshop on angels, that I did my first reading. I had not intended to participate in the workshop; Angel Wings had set up a display in the back of the room to sell angels. The workshop instructor was very insistent and persistent that she needed an additional person to assist her. In compliance, I went to the front of the class to do a reading on a woman there. When I closed my eyes, I saw muffins floating all around her energy field. I could see that she was taking the tops off the muffins and putting something inside them. I was told by the guides that when she baked, she infused love into her muffins and that she was well-loved and sought after for her work. She did indeed bake muffins for a living, and she also put pie filling inside them before they were baked. To my amazement, I was then asked by others to do readings on them. It was as if the universe opened up and said, "We knew you would awaken to your path; we have been waiting for you." I started offering my angel readings and mediumship inside Angel Wings.

In 2000, I invited another angel reader to teach classes on how to communicate with your angels and guides. The instructor wanted to know why I was not teaching the classes, and I told her I did not feel I was qualified. After all, what did I know about teaching? Again, the record in my head played, "Who do you think you are?" One stormy night, I had twelve people in the shop, and we were waiting for the instructor to arrive. I was surprised so many had shown up for the class. I called the instructor to see if she was okay and on her way. To my surprise, she was in the middle of a long, hot bubble bath and had totally forgotten the class. Her comment was, "I guess it is all up to you now." I did, indeed, teach this class and many classes after. My classes are called *Angels at Play*, and the angels had most assuredly decided that I needed to play that night.

There are so many ways in which we can communicate with our angels and guides. I often sit and do what is called automatic writing. I find my quiet space, and with my pen and paper, I ask a question. The question can be as simple as, "What do I need to know today, who is with me right now, or what should I do about a situation?" Sometimes the answer is instant, other times, it could take a while, but the angels will always answer you. You may not always like the answer, but if you trust your intuition, you will know it is the right answer for the situation.

In 2001 I asked my angel, "What do I do with my angel store and my readings?" I was doing 20 to 30 readings a week while running Angel Wings seven days a week. I was exhausted and knew that this was not what the universe wanted for me. It was one of those answers that I didn't like or understand, but I also knew it was the right answer. The angels told me that I was to turn my store purple. Angel Wings was done in a beautiful blue with cherub wallpaper; I loved the design and layout of the store. I asked them, "Why?" They told me that the new buyer liked purple. I called my friends and told them what the angels had said. My friends enthusiastically replied, "Let's do it!"

For the next two weeks, Angel Wings was in chaos, but in the end, it was a beautiful purple. Then I waited for months for the buyer. I was even given the name of the buyer, and at one point, someone with that name came to me and asked to purchase the store. I went back to my angels, and they informed me, "No, not her." I waited another few long months before a man wandered into the store looking at everything. I offered to assist him. He said he was in a state of confusion as he was retiring from his job and moving to Galesburg, a small town in Illinois that I most likely had never heard of. I started to laugh, as I had had a client phone consultation the night before from this very town. I asked him why he was moving. He told me that he and his wife had a dream of opening a store just like Angel Wings and there was a store in Galesburg for sale. I then inquired why they did not open a store in Gilbert, Arizona, which, I believe, is where he was from. He said he did not want to compete with Angel Wings, as he knew my store had become a destination for people from all over the world. It was at that time that I felt a slight push on my shoulder from my angel. I asked him what his wife's name was, and when he told me her name, I laughed—it was the name of the buyer that my angels had told me about. I asked if she liked purple, and he said her favorite color is purple, and her favorite song is "Lavender Blue." It wasn't until then that I told him my store was for sale. I moved on from Angel Wings in April of 2002 and continue, to this day, to do my angel readings and medium-ship work.

When I work with clients suffering the loss of a loved one, I am always guided by their loved one with a message that assures my client and communicates in a variety of ways. It could be white feathers, pennies, playing with the electricity, roses, hummingbirds, or even crickets. Always, the message is that they are loved. Sometimes the loved one shows me what they did in this lifetime or shows me their hobbies, verifying to my clients that the message is, indeed, from them.

Sometimes there is some confusion—a crossed path of sorts. A client once came to see me after the loss of her husband. During the reading, a motorcycle went past her energy field, not just once but twice. The second time, the motorcycle rider shouted to me to let his family know he was all right. I did not feel that this person belonged to my client, but I did inquire. She said no. That night I received a call from my best friend in Colorado, who informed me that his son-in-law had been struck and killed by a motorcycle after leaving a motorcycle show. You never know when or how the message will come in, but it will always be right.

We all have intuitive gifts. Some come in the form of a nudge, a song, automatic writing, gut feeling, a knowingness, or we see with something that others call our "third eye." It may be that you are guided to go right instead of left, or you are running late for work, when you are told to go back and double check that you turned off a burner, only to find it is all okay. On the way to work, you may pass a bad accident and realize that could have been you. Or, you may witness an exceptional sunrise that lifts you up. Talking to your angels is as easy as talking to a friend or writing a letter to a loved one—listening to your angels puts you on the best path. Angel Blessings!

CHAPTER

Four

The Gift Of Siloquia
By Dr. Vicki L. High

DR. VICKI L. HIGH

Dr. Vicki L. High is a multiple international best-selling author of *Heart 2 Heart Connections: Miracles All Around Us, When I Rise, I Thrive, Healer, Life Coach,* and *Inspirations.* She is the founder of Heart 2 Heart Healing, a Reiki Master Teacher, healing practitioner, life & business coach, counselor, speaker, minister, and former mayor. Dr. High, a pioneer in spiritual healing, boldly journeys into new frontiers of healing, love, and empowerment through

spiritual insights. She shares intuitive and experiential wisdom, connecting ideas and concepts, and creating patterns for life and healing. She lives through her heart, honoring each person as an aspect of God–Source. Vhigh4444@aol.com,
www.heart2heartconnections.us,
www.empowereddreams.com, @heart2heartprograms,
@stoptraumadrama, @kalmingkids,
@empowereddreams, @drvickilhigh.

Acknowledgments

I am so grateful to my family and friends, the mentors and teachers in my life, and the spiritual family that has sustained me through so many adventures! Special thanks to Diane Sellers, Tina & Lon Morgan, Mom for the gift of laughter and loving family, H2H Practitioners who continue to spread their unconditional love throughout the world, fellow contributing authors, Kyra & Todd Schaefer, and Janene, Jamie, Debbie, Darlene, and Ann for being great sounding boards. Thank you for your love and support!

The Gift Of Siloquia
By Dr. Vicki L. High

Supernatural Communication

One of the greatest blessings in my journey continues to be spiritual messages delivered by my "family of light." My messages come from angels, ascended masters, guides, and the great I Am. These supernatural messages shed light and new dimensions on the Heart 2 Heart Healing work and my purpose. I made a conscious choice to listen as they spoke through the vocal cords of a client on the table. Then I listened with child-like wonder, rather than run, thinking the person was possessed. I allowed the supernatural experience to unfold.

I hear remarkable truths that pertain to everyone and enlighten "whoever has ears, let them hear." Listen for the truth, because the truth is programmed into each heart. The information was channeled from a client, someone with channeling gifts, or directly through my heart, and changed my life. How do you explain seeing a client who doesn't know how to sign, start rapidly signing so fast that I can't follow what is being communicated? Clients spoke and sang in the "angelic language," but also English, Portuguese, and another language, possibly Aramaic. These clients didn't speak those languages. I am told, "People will listen and hear. They will come to their personal conclusions." What if you heard this message? "I Am. I Am all that has not been present. I Am who you have been waiting for. I Am all that is coming and all that will be. It is a birthing. It is a birthing of the new."

One client brought her family for a healing session. She began to speak as she lay on the massage table. There was a hushed expectancy in the room. Hannah's husband could not keep his eyes open and fell asleep on the couch. The ascended masters began to share insights and messages. It was exciting to touch the supernatural once again.

Gateways to Spirituality

"Gateway. Gateway. Gateway. This is a gateway–a gateway to spirituality." The words came from her mouth, but not from her consciousness. She was the vehicle for the message. Her words were accompanied by an amazing ballet using her graceful hands in gestures that had meanings that were beyond my comprehension. At some level, I felt I knew what these symbols meant. Her two hands were at her heart with fingertips touching and creating what looked like a church. Her hands came together, and you could hear her breathe an audible breath. Then it was almost like she was whistling. Then it became a whistle. She waved her hands in a spiral, crossing over and back, creating figure eights, infinity in sacred geometry. A sense of sacredness permeated the room.

Her toddler began to cry, and the baby was comforted by the voice, "Angel, it's okay. I know. You want to know where your mommy is. Who is this strange person here? Where's your Mommy? She's still here."

The voice then said to me. "She's scared. Sometimes when this happens, when children are afraid, they see what you don't see. You see a body. She sees me. She sees more than what you see. That's why she's afraid. But outside would be nice, if only for a moment." I picked the baby up, and we went outside. When we looked at the trees and grass, the colors seemed brighter—like a hazy film had been peeled away! When we came back in, she seemed calmer.

Then, The Voice came from Hannah and spoke to her husband and me.

"It's not often that I get these great and wonderful opportunities to speak to you. It's not often I get to speak to two wonderful people. For that, I am grateful.

"I am honored to truly be here today because I Am Who I Am. There is a communication between the physical and the supernatural. The supernatural is a realm that exists. You can smell it. You can feel it. It is hard to imagine because you are here. You are here on this earth plane. We are there. The two seem to bridge, but to the mind's eye, we are only a myth. We are there.

"Your existence is nothing without a level of love, a level of responsibility, a level of self-achievement, and a level of self-fulfillment. You cannot be any more than you think you can be. You were created to be in harmony. In disharmony, every cycle, every sense of self, every facet of your experience is disorganized. You are in peril. It is only up to you to bring everything together.

"We are always here. We will continue to be here, but our job is not to fix you. Our job is to guide you. It is to lead you. It is to instruct you. Your choices are yours. Your mind is yours. Your freedom is yours. Your harmony is yours. Your love is yours. Your disharmony is yours. I don't think

I can say it any clearer than I have. I hope you understand. Life is yours. It is as simple as that."

"And once you reach that area of your life, your existence will exceed the existence here. And once the existence is exceeded here, you must move on because your life's journey is ended. You have achieved. You have achieved self, spiritual self, loving thyself, owning thyself, and merging with spiritual and physical. Everything is one in harmony, and that is God!"

I could feel the strength that was building with every word and thought. The Voice continued, "I Am Who I Am. I say that with pride. I Am Who I Am."

"Your physical has no bearing on who you are. It is merely a shell. Once that shell is exposed—once that shell is unraveled, you are a spiritual being. I am a spiritual being. I am a spiritual being! I am a spiritual being because I Am. I Am Who I Am, get it? This shell, this body allows me to speak to you.

"It is physical. I Am spiritual. Physical and spiritual merge. When physical and spiritual merge, I can speak to you. Only can I interpret or only those who can interpret or hear me must be at a level of existence to hear me. It's easier for me to speak this way to you because I have a physical voice. I have a physical body. Therefore, the physical and the spiritual can communicate with you. That's what you are used to. That is why I can convey and say things to you, and you can hear me. Although this is not my voice, I can still speak to you. You can understand clearly what I am saying to you. It seems crazy, doesn't it? But, it's the truth. It is the truth, believe it or not! It is the truth."

Siloquia

"I guess you are wondering—why this person? Why that person? Why is this person able to? Why is Hannah able to? Why am I able to use her? Why am I able to use others? Why am I not able to use others? It is only a willingness. Let me explain this much. Some people in this world are born with signet programming before they get here. So, a person, for instance, someone like Hannah, I can use her easily—well, not easily, but I can come, and she is willing, by her choice, so I can speak through her. Before she got here, she was programmed as you say; she was given the ability to be a free vehicle, a free communication, a free gateway for spiritual and physical to connect. It's called—in Heaven (she pointed skyward)—siloquia. People with siloquia have the ability to communicate beyond earth, beyond the physical."

I asked, "Do I have this ability?"

"Yes. It's why you are here. If you weren't meant to be here, and you did not understand—if you were not gifted in this manner—there is no way you could sit here and listen to me speak to you. Not everyone can sit here and listen to me speak. Some people would be annoyed. Some people would be upset. Some people would think it's a hoax. Some people will think she's crazy. Everyone is crazy in this world, it seems, if you believe anything other than what is physical.

"There are layers and layers of existence. This is only one. Believe what you will, but there are others—other realms of your and my existence."

I asked, "Do you mean other planets—other worlds?"

"This planet and my planet, which we call Heaven, are far, but in between. Here is a place—we know we are here on Earth. This is what you see. This is where you exist. This is how you breathe—what you are. There is what I Am—a true spiritual being. Now, how close are they? They connect. They touch, but to the physical eye, it is often hard to connect. It is often hard to see. Why is it hard to see? If you saw everything in spirit, there would be no need for you to live in the natural. It would be extremely challenging for you to complete your journey.

"Now true, there are others. There are individuals with the ability to see us. That is their purpose. That is their calling. There is no problem with that. But the true reason as to why the spiritual doors of your eyes are not continuously open is because, as with anything in this world, it can become a distraction for you in your journey. Your journey is to complete your purpose."

I asked, "Is my purpose unconditional love and healing?"

"Absolutely! That is part of it, but there are so many different levels of love and healing, as you know. Healing is not only of the spirit, it's who you are. Healing is. It leaks from every sense of who you are. Love is. Love is the key to everything! You cannot exist in harmony without love— God. It seems so simple. Yet, it is so difficult for others to hold onto—love of self, love for others, love. Love is love. Do you have any questions?"

I responded, "I have a million of them. Why is it so hard for people to understand how sacred and spiritual this work is? Why do they assume it cannot be from Jesus and God?"

"What you have to realize is that their box is not your box. Their mission is not your mission. 'For God so loved the world, He gave His only begotten Son.' Now, when you look at people and what they feel, how they exist, you must realize that they are in an area of their life where some are transforming, some are changing, but others are not. How can you reach them? That is difficult alone.

"Your job is to exist, but not allow others to keep you from existing. When you give of yourself, when you show what you have to others, it is simple. They take it, or they leave it. It is not your job to prove or reason. It is only your job to exist in what you are here to do. It is a continuous struggle to reach others, why? Because others are closed-minded. They exist only in the now, and they believe only what they see. Some never get it. But the important thing is that you get it, and by you getting it, you are an example to others. So, you must live according to what you feel is appropriate. What is the right thing for you to do for you? Allow yourself to be exactly who you are, leaving all unnecessary stuff, junk, fog, and conditioning behind. Being you is all we ask of you.

"Changing others is sometimes an unfavorable task. We tried. We failed. But yes, you are on the right path. You are on the right journey, although it seems especially difficult at times. You've got to keep on keeping on. You have to say to yourself that you are going to see this through no matter what and trust that.

"It's always a joy to share the wonders of the world, to speak truth, to speak highly of what you know—what you love to do. It's always a pleasure for us to see you do that.

But it can also be a disappointing task when you don't get the results that you want. It's important to have a strong distinction of what is expected of yourself and what you simply cannot control. Sometimes you must let go. Simply raise up your hands and say you've done your part and be happy and content with that. Although it may seem challenging, it is up to you to stay in constant harmony within self. Don't allow anything to hinder your progress.

"Part of your mission is to fill the void within self. Again, reaching self-harmony, loving thyself. It all comes together—the spiritual and the physical. You have God's grace. You have things that no one can truly understand. You are love. Don't ever let anyone take that away from you. They simply cannot. Do not give of yourself to injure yourself. Love thyself first and foremost, and the rest will come.

"You have to realize that you are evolving. You are continuously changing. That's why things seem not to last. They come. They go. Because to a person who is evolving, who is trying to reach their True Self, who is changing, things come in and go out. Because that is what you need at this juncture of your life. It's not bad luck. It's not that God doesn't love you, or because things are too difficult, or that at any point in your life, you won't make it. You are continuously changing. To change, you must evolve. To evolve, things have to evolve around you quickly."

"Most importantly, we want you to listen—listen to your heart—listen to us. Don't make any rash decisions. Don't feel that you must make an instant decision, no matter what situation you're in. There's always another opportunity. There's always another way. We want you to simply do the work."

The information shared during these encounters is amazing. There have been dozens, perhaps hundreds, of messages with insights and mysteries that changed my life and how I exist in the world. Even when I reread the messages, new insights are unveiled as if the information has layers and levels that I understand as I progress through my journey. My gift of siloquia enables me to hear these messages, and I am eternally grateful. I believe communicating with the supernatural is truly our divine heritage. Your journey is yours alone. I invite you to experience the grand adventure of your divine sovereignty. Are you ready?

CHAPTER

Five

Teachings From The Angels
And My Guides
By Chantal Fortin

CHANTAL FORTIN

Chantal Fortin is a mother, grandmother, sister, friend, teacher, soul sister, and twin soul. The heart unites her with her loving, kind-hearted soul mate. She has known about her exceptional abilities and has been receiving teachings from her guides and angels since a young age. Her ability to communicate with passed ones, which is a gift sent from Heaven, needs to be taught and shared. Through intuitive readings, coaching, and past life regressions, she connects and heals when her guides and angels instruct her to do so.

Now that she has more time and years of experience, and finds herself to be where she should be on this earthly journey, it is time to share her gift on a grander scale through this book. You can reach Chantal Fortin on her Facebook page Chantal Fortin -Spiritual Journeying or by email at regressions44@hotmail.com.

Acknowledgments

I give my sincere recognition to my children and their beautiful families for accepting a mother and grandmother who is different on many levels. I reciprocate their unconditional love. To my soul sisters and twin soul who share with me these experiences and visions, I am forever grateful. My soulmate, my patient and tender love, I appreciate your understanding as well as your continuous encouragement and support. To my beautiful earthly family and friends, I have immense gratitude for you believing in me. My family in Heaven—parents, grandparents, relatives, and friends—as well as angels and guides, complement me on this earthly journey. With incredible and precise guidance, I share this gift I have received and developed to the point of now being able to share it. Without all of you, I wouldn't be the person that I am today. I am truly blessed!

Teachings From The Angels
And My Guides
By Chantal Fortin

It is now time to share my gift. I am not a writer. However, I feel the urge to write; it consumes me. I sit at my computer, and I start typing what comes through me. When I stop writing, I am thankful for the bouts of energy that passed through me like surges with messages from the angels and my guides. I am grateful for every word written. I continue living my ordinary life until the next bout of energy or spiritual experience. I have sincere gratitude for my gift, and now it is time to begin sharing and teaching through this book.

On a daily basis, I am constantly surrounded and interacting with the angels and my guides. For example, on a cold Monday morning, my soulmate had to leave at five o'clock a.m. to be on time at a job site. However, he couldn't find his keys. I could hear him going through the house, searching in his pockets and other places for his keys. I received the image of his keys on the ground outside in front of the garage door. I also got the message from his guardian angel that he couldn't find his keys because he was not looking outside where they were. I got up and told him where they were. He looked at me and went to look outside. While still in bed, I could see the image of where he was looking, and it was nowhere close to the keys. I opened the door and told him to look in front of the garage. Again, he was closer to his snow machine, which he said he had worked on during the weekend. It was cold outside. I put on my big boots, and my giant winter coat over my nightgown walked outside. Ten steps later, I was pointing at my feet where the keys were. The look on his face was like he had seen a ghost.

How it All Began

I remember being conscious of traveling in the cosmos when I was three or four years old. I could not recognize where I was, but I knew that one day, I would know where I was traveling to and why. I only found out much later, at 25 years old to be exact. I remember knowing things at a young age, but not knowing how I knew these facts, or why I knew so much that others didn't seem to know or understand.

The first time I realized I was truly blessed by embarking on this angelic journey was in 1991. I was a young mother, and my son was six months old. I was enjoying motherhood to the fullest in our century-old paternal house. One day in early July, I woke up suddenly with the feeling that I was being watched. As I opened my eyes, I saw a beautiful older woman smiling and standing at the foot of our bed. It was five o'clock a.m. At second glance, the woman looked like she was made up of misty particles. She was almost as bright as a physical person. I wasn't scared. It was my first time seeing a ghost, a spirit, or someone who had passed on to the other plane, I wasn't sure. I asked her who she was. I couldn't recognize her. She smiled at me and told me she was visiting the house. I panicked—why would a person who has passed on appear in front of me?

I thought she had a message for me that my son was in danger. I ran to his bedroom. He was sleeping in his crib; he was still breathing. "There must be a fire in the house," I thought. I ran through the sizeable three-story farmhouse. No fire. I went back to my son's room. I picked him up in my arms. He was healthy and breathing. I now noticed this lady was following me through the house. She was with me in my son's bedroom. She had a beautiful energy surrounding her. I wasn't scared. It was almost calming to be surrounded by her. By now, I was feeling a calm, soothing, warm energy take over me. I felt safe and that my son was protected by this loving motherly angel. She was a great-grandmother who had lived in this house with her family. I went back to sleep with this warm, fuzzy feeling of unconditional love. I was never the same again. From then on, I felt a mystical awakening taking place within myself. My intuition was developing at a fantastic rate. I would receive more knowledge and information. For a long time, I keep this secret to myself, because I was never sure why I was receiving this information from a cosmos source, nor did I know how to share it.

A Birth in Heaven

Throughout the years, I've received numerous visits from my beautiful, passed-on great-grandmother. She has taught me many lessons about life and the spiritual world. I am fortunate, and now realize that I have this angelic energy surrounding me. Her first visit, described in the above paragraph, was only a few hours before her brother was to leave the earth world. She came over for a visit to the house she used to live in. She later told me that following her appearance, she joined loved ones and angels to welcome her brother into the spirit world. To us humans, our great-uncle died, but for the deceased loved ones and the angels, it was a birth in Heaven. My loving great-grandmother described this birth into the spirit world with such beauty and splendor that it changed me forever. However sad as it is to lose a loved one, I cannot help but remember the image I received of the birth in Heaven with all of its love and splendor. Where all of this new spirit's deceased loved ones and many angels were waiting for him to arrive. The gathering and the greetings he received upon arrival into Heaven were terrific. He was immediately wrapped in waves of warmth and loving energies. Angels were singing and beautiful music could be felt. Incredible beauty was all around, and light penetrated through the thick, voluminous clouds. The vibrating power of the spiritual newborn body as it was being carried by angels through this gathering. I could feel the divine energy. However, I always wonder how limited is my human body in terms of understanding and feeling all of this angelic splendor. I am also at loss for the word to describe what I am shown, and to translate and explain the messages I receive. Birth in Heaven is a beautiful phenomenon. It is the return to the state where you are connected to all your loved ones, both physically on earth and in the spiritual world. However, for us humans, based on our reality, it is a sad event called death.

Communication with Loved Ones

I received numerous teachings about angels and the spiritual world throughout the years. Some I have asked for, while most of the teachings were given to me like gifts. I received each of these at specific moments in various forms for different reasons.

The one teaching that I will elaborate on is communication with loved ones who are now in Heaven. Angels help us communicate with our deceased loved ones. As humans, we are social beings. We communicate on a daily basis. It is this lack of communication and the actual physical connection that is broken when someone passes on to the spiritual world. When our loved ones leave their earthly physical body to enter the spiritual plane, they are born in Heaven. We, as humans, through our physical body, with our eyes and hands, cannot see or touch our spirit loved one anymore. To get in touch with them, we need to elevate our vibrations and adapt our means of communication. We have that capacity. The human body, when trained to do so, can communicate through energies. I have received many teachings from my guides and angels this way. I have also practiced this wonderful gift over the years. It is now the time for me to share this with you. There are lessons and exercises below if you wish to deepen your communication skills and establish contact with your deceased loved ones and the angels. It will take practice and time. However, the journey will be well worth it throughout its course.

Lesson 1

We are so used to having a cell phone, that we no longer send human telepathic signals. We no longer listen to our body for messages. Our human brain can do so much more than we can imagine. Most of us have not used telepathic communication, nor have we developed this sense. However, on the occasion when we do get a feeling or a message, we are stunned and think it was a coincidence that we were thinking of the person and they sent us a message. You are communicating telepathically without acknowledging it.

Imagine how training to communicate telepathically could further awaken this sense as our ancestor were able to do at different times during evolution. I have guided and brought people to this conscious state of mental awareness on individual bases. Telepathic communication can be developed. The human brain is fantastic; it knows things and can perform tasks that the conscious self is not fully aware of.

Practice these exercises to communicate telepathically, and journal your results:

- Daily, preferably at the same time everyday practice for ten to fifteen minutes at a time.

- Start with only five minutes the first time, and increase as you get used to it.

- Mornings are usually better because you are fresh, and your mind is clearer of thought, however, choose a time during the day when you have tranquility, are more relaxed, and are in a clear state of mind for excellent comm-unications.

Telepathic practice if your loved one is still on the earth and conscious:

If you have a sick loved one and that person is willing to practice telepathic communication with you, start the exercises as described above. Let the energies flow when you are both in the same room, or while you are both on the phone or a visual call, if you are at a distance. Practice these exercises with your loved one for at least seven to ten days.

- After a while, you will start feeling the connection, and you will actually feel yourself reading the other person's mind when you look into their eyes or just by thinking about them. This is the point where you are both opened up and willing to share images, emotions, and to communicate.

- At this point, distance yourselves; however, continue to practice together at the same time. Once this flow is established at a distance, it is then time to practice this communication periodically at different intervals during the day by trying to get the other person's attention. Check the time when you receive a message or think about the other person, or call to check if they were trying to get your attention. Gauge your success and continue practicing. You have this ability; it is within you.

Telepathic communication with deceased loved ones:

- Practice telepathic communication, as described above. However, to get confirmation that you are communicating and feeling the energies with your loved one, you will have to periodically ask for signs from the angels.

- Signs from the angels can be related to the person you are communicating with, such as a butterfly, a bird, a dime, a specific person you will hear from, and so on. You will eventually get the feeling and see the sign as a confirmation. These are winks from our loved ones in Heaven.

In the same way, you practiced communicating with loved ones, you can communicate with the angels. Work with your angels; they participate in these exchanges. They open the lines of communication for us, and they signal us to listen. There are no coincidences. Every sign is there and happens for a reason.

The key to happiness is to live with passion

Another one of those teachings was given to me while I was at an amusement park with my daughter and my niece. I was waiting for the girls to come off of a ride, when I noticed a middle-aged lady also waiting at the ride exit with an empty wheelchair. When the amusement ride was finished, she proceeded closer to the door to pick up a fragile, preteen boy. He had a fantastic smile and was joined by three other young happy, energetic preteens. They were all helping the frail boy into the wheelchair and together deciding where they would go next. The park was large with lots of people. I let my daughter and her cousin choose which ride they wanted next. Amazingly enough, I always ended up waiting for my girls beside this lady with the empty wheelchair. She had fantastic energy and a contagious smile. We started talking. Her son had a degenerative disease. She had four children, two who had been afflicted with this disease, and two healthy children. Her oldest son had succumbed to this disease a few years ago. Her second son was now in his final years on earth. Doctors had given him only a few weeks to live during the winter, but his mother kept on telling him that she would take him and his cousins to the park as soon as it opened in the spring. She told me that his wish for this special day had kept him alive for months. This amazing lady with her special son were having the time of their lives. They were on my path for me to receive this lesson from Heaven: Enjoy every day as if it were your last.

Lesson 2

Set goals, real goals, and live your life to the fullest based on these goals. Do not let anything get in the way or put you down. Push yourself and strive to live your life like it was through the eyes of a child going to the amusement park. Raise your energies and see the world with the passion of a child.

I thank you sincerely for your time reading this chapter. Please reach out to me to let me know how these exercises have helped you communicate with your loved ones on this earth and those who have passed on. I am presently working on a book with full lessons on how to practice communications with living and/or passed on loved ones, angels, and guides. There will also be other books to follow, I am told.

CHAPTER

Six

Flower Garden, Not So Much
By Debbie Helsel

DEBBIE HELSEL

Debbie is a Heart 2 Heart Healing and Heart 2 Heart Connections Practitioner. While additionally trained in Reconnective Healing, Reiki, Spiritual Response Therapy, Rose Alchemy, with some study of flower essences and essential oils, she also works with her guides and angels seeking divine guidance on healing with crystals, mostly through self-study and discovery. She has a Doctorate of Metaphysical Studies through The Alliance of Divine Love Ministry, and studies with the Center for Healing in Orlando, Florida. She enjoys digging crystals and attending drum circles.

Debbie is the Executive Director at Back to Nature Wildlife Refuge & Education Center in Orlando. Since 1990, Debbie has dedicated her life as a federal and state licensed wildlife rehabilitator caring for injured and orphaned wildlife, and also as a public educator, and is currently on the board of the Florida Wildlife Rehabilitator's Association.
www.BTNwildlife.org BTNdebbie@gmail.com

Acknowledgments

Thank you to Kyra and As You Wish Publishing for the opportunity to become a published artist. You are an angel and inspire so many of us to achieve lifelong dreams! Thank you to God, my angels, and guides for trusting, loving, and teaching me, and to Mother Earth for all that you are and allowing me to be your steward. Thank you to Megan Elliott, my dear friend and editor, Rev. Stephanie Josephs, Mandy Freeman, and Ms. Bev at Spiral Circle for showing me a path of spiritual growth, Diana Ewald and Pillars of Light for my beloved spiritual garden, ADL Ministry and Center for Healing for teaching and guiding me, Nancy Kott, my seventh-grade science teacher and my friend, for instilling your passion in me to love the environment and life's creatures, and "B" (you know who you are) and my family—thank you for a lifetime of support.

Flower Garden, Not So Much
By Debbie Helsel

I feel we are watched over and taught our entire lives by those who I believe to be angels, teachers, and guides. It can take many years for this to be recognized and embraced, if ever, by some. I think back on my years and know that they have been with me, with lessons every step of the way. When I was less than one-and-a-half years old, I fell from a second story while I was watching the cows at my uncle's farm. I landed in my cousins' sandbox, and I was told afterward that everyone thought I was dead. I had a broken leg and still bear the scar to this day. I only recently was shown that Archangel Michael was there and caught me, setting me to rest on the ground, minimizing my injuries and sparing my life for a higher purpose. I didn't know that much about the angels and guides when I was younger, but I did know that even attending church was emotionally over-whelming for me, and it was difficult to go, which still happens to this day. I don't remember most of the sermons, but I do remember how emotional I would get. It made me uncomfortable to be so vulnerable in front of people in that particular setting, so I quit going, except on occasion.

I think this is why God gave me a different path—one that connected me to the animals and assured that my vulnerabilities are seen and can be expressed easily without judgment, where my emotions are what they are. I've been accused in the past by a few who thought I made up my emotions to have a greater impact. But if you knew me, you'd know I am as genuine as they come. Maybe this is why

I was gifted by the heavens with spiritual space and boundless opportunities to connect in a different way. I was molested by a neighbor as a child and was almost raped when I was in high school. I still have battle scars from my first relationship, and I've carried baggage that few people know about—including my family, until this moment—and I still work to heal from it. I consistently work to let it go, while finding forgiveness for them and myself for letting it hold me back. I know that the angels have been working with me on it for years, through many avenues, along with my minimes. It has helped me talk more freely about it. It's hard work, but worth it to free myself.

Years ago, there was a place that held channeling circles in Winter Park, Florida, called Pillars of Light. I was still fairly new to my spiritual journey; I was open to seeking out new spiritual experiences and this was on my list of to-dos. It felt like a fun night out for some entertainment, but it turned out to be surprisingly real for me. The channeling circles were in a group setting and the facilitator, who came from another part of the state, would have group and individual messages. I wanted to figure out the process and outthink what was going to happen, trying to decide for myself if what was happening was real or merely someone out to make a buck—but it sounded like fun anyway.

Right away, I knew something was happening, and it was exciting because it was my first experience with seeing actual energies like this! I watched as the energy of the facilitator would leave through her crown, then the individual guides entered through her crown, and I watched them leave as others came in, until all the readings were done and her energy came back into her body. I could see the guides' energies enter and leave through her crown, and the others in the room couldn't! Wow, how cool is that? It was fascinating and intriguing for me. Although I had some training in seeing auras, it didn't usually come easily for me, and I had never experienced something like this before.

I attended the circles frequently, and it seemed that the guides that came through for me regularly suggested I plant flowers. My guides were typically the same ones, and the energies were consistent with when I had originally met them, so I was confident that my interactions were real for me. After being asked to plant flowers, I wanted to test the waters. One day I tore up the backyard and figured I would answer their challenge; then, if this was all real, they would stop asking or acknowledge "my garden" as I lovingly call it. I had absolutely no idea that it would become anything but a flower garden. I have never shared this story on such a public level before, and most people that know me have no idea of this story. Looking back at my timeline, my garden began within a week of the Lunar Eclipse and Harmonic Concordance galactic alignment in November of 2003.

I used a pendulum as my tool for this project, which I had gotten recently from my favorite spiritual book store, Spiral Circle, and was learning to use. As I tore the yard up, I went ,for some reason, in a circular pattern, and it turned out to be almost exactly perfect based on my answers of guidance. There were directions, but not typical directions, so I stood in where I was led to be as the center, and I turned in a circle until I was directed to stop. I walked from that center point to the edge, and it also stopped at the boundary of the original circle. This happened four times, and before I knew it, I had created an outline in my backyard—a circle that now had a peace sign within it. I was floored and super excited. I was in love with my garden and obsessed with what was coming next. The center line of the peace sign went directionally straight to the door of the screened porch. There were crystals placed at certain depths and directions and in certain places, and numerous other things were added as I received guidance. I know I have been protected by the angels my whole life and I only work with beings of the light, so I knew that I was safe, and that the highest divine guidance was in play here.

This became my spiritual space, my temple, I guess. As I was digging it up originally, there was a Native American medicine man dancing and chanting in the garden with me. He was praying and blessing the space. I could see him clear as day, but no one else ever did. This to me was my assurance that the wisdom and the guidance I would receive was clearly from a higher power, and being part Native American myself, I wasn't surprised that my ancestors came to help too. The angels and fairies came, along with the teachers and guides who hung out too. Over time, I stopped using the pendulum and recognized that I was receiving messages in other ways, merely by opening my heart to receive. I spent a lot of time listening from within, and I would hear them speaking to me. I had a difficult time shutting the work chatter off in my brain so I could be in a space to receive messages and inspiration. When I step in my garden, it is like stepping into another world, and nothing else matters in that moment, almost like my personal mystery school. The energy has evolved and grown beyond what I would have ever imagined, and it continues to grow.

The angels told me that people would heal through the garden, although I wasn't sure how that would happen. This was my sacred space; I am not a party person or a home entertainer, and am fairly reclusive and private when I am not at work. So I wasn't sure what that would mean, or how it was supposed to happen. I have done only a few healings inside the garden over all these years, although I have shared my garden with several healers and close friends. On a few occasions, I have opened the house up for energy healings, done private healing sessions, and facilitated Heart 2 Heart classes as well. Frequently, I am given divine guidance and messages for those on my table, not every time, but sometimes quite profound information, mostly to the client. A lot of my various crystals ask to take part in the healings, and I am always only too happy to have their assistance.

There has always been more to it, and the angels consistently utilize me as a conduit to be of service, which I am humbled and excited about. As I was searching at pow-wows and other places for the crystals for my garden, I learned that I could actually go and dig crystals myself! I was excited and learned all that I could, before taking my first journey to Arkansas to dig for quartz. I was immediately addicted. I made sure to ask for assistance from the crystals and stones, requesting that if there were any that wanted to come back with me, or if there was someone they needed me to take them to, they needed to present themselves to me somehow—which they have always done.

All of the crystals that I've brought back from my digs have gone in the garden before leaving on their journey. Quite a few of them have spoken to me directly and asked me to take them to a certain person. Yes, at first, I felt like I was crazy, but it was such a blessing that they chose me, and I was hearing them speak. I asked to be of service, and they were holding me to task, with an additional element of awesomeness. The crystals were to be in the garden before I delivered them to their destination, so that the energies of the garden and the access to the portal there would always be accessible to the crystal, wherever it was. They chose their path, not I. I am a crystal keeper who helps get crystals to their person or destination when they tell me it's time to go. I know the crystals are not all meant to be with me, which is why it is all okay. I follow my path of service and listen to my intuition and my angels, teachers, and guides, letting go of what I think is supposed to happen and trusting that it is all in divine order as it should be.

My garden has been inspirational, as well as healing for me, teaching me to trust my inner guidance and listen with an open heart and mind. It is my sanctuary where I can listen and hear when God speaks. I have received consistent messages for myself and others, and have helped others heal on some level that was needed. It has also been a place of letting go of that which doesn't serve me, or others, any longer. Those painful memories, tragedies, and past hurts that felt like they cut so deep that I could never get past them, have lessened or become neutral in their energetic hold on me. So my garden isn't only for helping everyone else; it has been for my healing as well, on a high level, and it was my backyard that has evolved for many years into my personal sacred space.

Being an earth keeper, it is my duty to listen to the messages and do my part to care for our Mother Earth. I listen to guidance with an open heart, and aide the elementals in protecting her, along with all the teachers, guides, and angels that are on this mission with me.

Being open to service is a conscious choice and can have a million meanings. Many have already made choices, and are following paths that will help raise vibrations and empower others to become their best selves. You have to trust and be willing to let go of what you think you know, and allow God, the angels, teachers, and guides to work with and through you for the best and highest good of all. I did not know I would have the intimate relationship with them all that I do have, and that it would come in one of the most unlikely ways. After all, I thought I was planting a flower garden, and just so you know, I never got flowers to grow in it, only a rosemary plant and a wonderful oak tree that the squirrels planted for me. The rest is rocks, stones, and crystals, along with a fire pit for energetic fires (not real fires), and numerous spiritual items. It can be quite easy to create a sacred space for yourself if you are open it, but know the possibility of being called to service through it.

You can try one of these for insight:

- Set aside some quiet time that is yours alone, without distractions, so that you can simply be in the moment.
- Find a place that is yours, one that feels right—some kind of quiet space—and have a pen and a journal close by. Sometimes drums or meditative music, listening to sounds of nature may help to get you in the gap. Write what you hear, even if right now it doesn't make sense.

• Outdoors is a great place as you are away from electronics (the most you can) and can be present and in the now. It can be easier to connect than when you are inside with potential distractions.

• Maybe close your eyes, be silent and listen with your heart. You may see pictures in your mind, you may hear conversation in your head, try to write down what you can remember or record it and come back and listen later while asking for clarity.

• The space doesn't have to be a large area and can be as simple as having a bench, where they can sit with you. It could be under a tree, in a kayak, on a dock near a lake, on a back porch, or even on a daily walk. It is similar to meditating.

• Your sacred space can be as easy as your energy bubble around you, or it can be a physical place, or on a walk.

• Don't overthink it, and be open to what messages come through.

CHAPTER

Seven

Connecting With Your Archangels Through Color By Debbie Labinski

DEBBIE LABINSKI

Debbie Labinski is an angel communicator, intuitive personal stylist, inspirational online speaker, spiritual teacher, and author in seven multi-author books. She helps women who are struggling with practical and fun ways to connect with the archangels through color and creating their perfect wardrobe. Her passion is to help all women connect with their true style, while also learning about how angels vibrate in colors and how joining the two together will support a more meaningful and joyful life. You can reach Debbie at Debbielabinski.com, and by email at debbielabinski@gmail.com. Follow her on Facebook @debbielabinskiangelsandstyling and Instagram @joyfulangelintuitivestylist to connect on a daily basis.

Acknowledgments

I must thank and acknowledge my family, my angels, and my supportive friends for all the love and patience while writing this amazing angel chapter. I have learned so much over the last six years about how to connect with angels, and I want to thank the many mentors and teachers that have taught me to believe in angels and in my dreams. Thank you to my two editors, Kendra and Kristine—you made this writing experience so much fun and helped me to tap into my most memorable angel experiences. You two offered me guidance on ways to express my words so that people will connect with my stories. Thank you Kyra and Todd Schaefer for offering authors a place to share our experiences! I am so excited for this book to be shared with the world!

Connecting With Your Archangels Through Color
By Debbie Labinski

In 2014, I prayed for something to change my awareness—something or someone to teach me how to heal and love myself again. I felt ready to look outside of church and my current relationships to truly find myself. I had given birth to three children who brought light and meaning to my life in a fulfilling way, but I was suffering from weight gain, depression, and loneliness. I started reading about angels, joining energy circles, and taking intuition and angel classes. I felt my life shift when I started to connect to the archangels through meditation, automatic writing, and wearing the colors that the archangels vibrate to.

Within months of inviting the archangels into my day, it became clear to me and others around me, that this was exactly what I needed to be doing. Within two years, I felt ready to share my gifts with others, and started offering readings and teaching intuition classes to women who also wanted to learn to connect with archangels in a unique and fun way. I learned how much I love to teach people about these magical, amazing light-beings that are here to support us, guide us, and connect us to our higher selves.

Throughout the Holy Bible, there are seven main archangels and seven days in a week. The idea of assigning an angel color to each of those days, beginning with Monday all the way through Sunday, became a fun and easy way to become familiar with each of the archangels' vibrations.

Have you noticed that every color carries an individual vibrational energy? When you are wearing a color, you are creating a vibrational energy that archangels can connect with. It is like wearing a protective cloak that speeds up the vibrational pull between you and that archangel. I invite you to focus your daily outfit choices, prayers, and intentions on a different angel color vibration, to help you remember that your angels are with you, supporting you in your day and in different areas of your life.

I am going to introduce you to five of my favorite archangels and their color vibrations. You will learn how the archangels wish to support you, and which colors they resonate with, followed by an invitation to call in their energy and an affirmation. I encourage you to journal your angel experiences at the end of each day to remind you how miraculous each connection is, how you felt during the connection, and what you were wearing that deepened or strengthened your connection with your daily archangel.

Archangel Michael

Archangel Michael vibrates to the color blue, his energy is known for strength, protection, and supporting you with your life purpose. Wearing blue when you invite Archangel Michael to connect will support you when you're feeling weak, scared, or feel like you have wandered off of your life path. Archangel Michael's energy is such a powerful feeling to have flow through you.

My encounter with Archangel Michael was during a difficult time in my life when I needed strength and courage. I invited Archangel Michael to connect to me physically, and within minutes, I felt a powerful whoosh. I wanted to have the experience of seeing him, so I grabbed my camera to take a picture, the flash came back at me, and through my camera lens, I saw a blue light completely take over the space, followed by a white orb stream, and it was like nothing I had ever seen before. I felt loved, safe, and in awe of this spiritual confirmation that angels do exist. I will always treasure my connection with Archangel Michael.

When you are in need of strength and courage, wear your favorite blue, and invite Archangel Michael to support you.

Dear Archangel Michael, please surround me in your blue light of protection and strength. Help me to see myself safe, hear your words that create feelings of unconditional love, and feel the comforting warmth of your wings surrounding me, while knowing that my desire to move forward and stay focused on my true life purpose is being granted. Thank you, God, thank you, Archangel Michael—I know that you are with me—and so it is.

Affirmation for wearing blue with Archangel Michael: I am fully protected in life, and truly feel the balance I deserve.

Archangel Jophiel

When Archangel Jophiel's energy is invited into your day, she will help you find joy, see beauty, and increase your creativity. Archangel Jophiel's energy can vibrate to the color yellow or hot pink. When you need to see the beauty of life or the beauty of a situation you are working through, hot pink will be supportive of your connection to Archangel Jophiel. When joy is lacking in your life or needs a boost, this would be a great time to wear yellow and invite Archangel Jophiel to join you in your day.

My experience with Archangel Jophiel became strongest when I gained weight after my third child. I was thirty-six and have always had confidence in my appearance and style. I found myself lacking joy when looking in the mirror and discovering that my clothes no longer supported me in feeling joyful and beautiful. I called on Archangel Jophiel when I needed help in adjusting my style, selecting clothing, and assembling outfits that felt authentic to the woman I have become.

When you seek joy, beauty, and creativity, wear your favorite yellow or hot pink, and invite Archangel Jophiel to support you.

Dear Archangel Jophiel, I invite you to connect to my inner spirit. Please help me to embrace my creativity, and to increase my ability to see the joy that life has to offer me through my ages and stages. I am grateful for your support and vibrational energy during this time of need. Thank you, God, thank you, Archangel Jophiel, and so it is.

Affirmation for wearing yellow with Archangel Jophiel: I see, feel, and spread joy in all that I do.

Affirmation for wearing hot pink with Archangel Jophiel: I am the beauty that I desire to see in the world around me.

Archangel Raphael

Archangel Raphael is known as the healing angel of mind, body, and spirit. His energy, when invited, will support you with attracting a healing mindset throughout your day. Wearing the vibrations of the color green will support you in feeling a stronger connection to Archangel Raphael, and can help you to attract new healing opportunities, possibilities, and people that could shift your healing journey.

My first introduction to Archangel Raphael was when I realized that I needed help with my weight. I discovered when wearing the color bright green, I felt closer to his vibration of healing energy. I was seeking this connection to Archangel Raphael to help me create a sense of trust that all is well with my body. Archangel Raphael guided me to become a Reiki practitioner, introduced me to essential oils that support my emotional and physical well-being, and motivates me to acknowledge my emotions and trust that I am safe to feel them instead of stuffing them away.

When you need to increase your personal healing abilities, wear your favorite color green and invite Archangel Raphael to support you.

Dear Archangel Raphael, I invite you to connect to my mind, body, and my inner spirit. I am in need of your healing green energy to flow through me and cleanse all the toxic thoughts, foods, and feelings from my body that have created my ailments. I know that you are here to support my emotions that I stuffed away, and are creating a safe place in life for me to heal myself. Thank you, God, thank you, Archangel Raphael, and so it is.

Affirmation for wearing green with Archangel Raphael: I believe in my healing abilities, and I trust my life reflects the healing I desire.

Archangel Uriel

Archangel Uriel vibrates to the color red. Call on Archangel Uriel when you are walking through a negative experience and need spiritual guidance and answers. When you wear red, you will connect to his energy and experience lightness and receive inspiration that will support you in transmuting the negativity of your present and past experiences.

Archangel Uriel directed me in seeing a job advertisement for a company that I believed in wholeheartedly. I had been wearing red and connecting to him regularly, asking for a job that supported me with feeling valuable and offered flexibility with my family's schedule. I had been hoping and wishing for over a year for this opportunity to arrive, and I wore red for the job interview. I happily received an offer and took it without hesitation, knowing this was a gift from Archangel Uriel.

When in need of transmutation energy, wearing your favorite red will support you and invite Archangel Uriel into your day.

Dear Archangel Uriel, I invite you to support me in transmuting any fearful energy that blocks me from seeing my light and my true value. I know that I am here to serve with ideas, creativity, and authenticity, which will help other people see their personal value. Thank you, God, thank you, Archangel Uriel, and so it is.

Affirmation for wearing red with Archangel Uriel: I am my own authority. I truly believe in my ability to share my passion with the world and make a difference.

Archangel Chamuel

Archangel Chamuel vibrates to the color pink. Call on Archangel Chamuel when self-love becomes a struggle, and the relationships you seek are feeling distant. Archangel Chamuel will support you in feeling worthy of love, and see the love in others being reflected back at you with grace. When you wear pink, you will connect to her energy and experience a loving embrace that creates a sense of belonging in your body and relationship with your higher self and others. You may receive inspiration that will support you in dressing the person you are today and let go of any self-doubt of your value and beauty that you are here to offer the world.

Archangel Chamuel showed up for us one day on the way to school. I was sharing with my boys how to invite Archangel Chamuel into our day. We were asking Chamuel to help us to have love for others who may be challenging to love and to love ourselves in these situations. Within seconds of this angel invitation, a car smashed into our car while at a red light. Thank goodness we were all unharmed, despite the fact that she was going 70 miles per hour. I found myself questioning why this happened to us, especially after we had prayed for protection. Were we not deserving of protection? Why did Archangel Chamuel let this driver hit us and total our car? Archangel Chamuel answered me through my friends. She said, "You were protected, this is how you were able to walk away from this terrible accident unharmed." Archangel Chamuel helped me to find compassion for the driver, even though she was the catalyst of this traumatic experience for each of us. Archangel Chamuel supported my boys and me every step of the way with unconditional love, and helped me overcome the fears that the accident created within me.

When in need of self-love energy, wearing your favorite pink will support you and invite Archangel Chamuel into your day.

Dear Archangel Chamuel, I call upon you to connect to my heart and shine your loving light within me. Please help me to see love in all that is around me, help me to receive that love from others. I know that I am here to experience unconditional loving relationships, and you are here to bring those opportunities of love to my awareness, so that we all, as a collective, can learn what unconditional love feels like. Archangel Chamuel, please help me to exude these loving vibrations out to the world, and shift the energy in the spaces that I occupy. Thank you, God, thank you, Archangel Chamuel, and so it is.

Affirmation for wearing pink with Archangel Chamuel: I am open to receive unconditional love, and I truly believe I am deserving of feeling and experiencing self-love every day.

Archangel Signs

Archangel signs and repeating numbers show up when you least expect it. I have had hundreds of experiences, and so can you. Archangels have been known to use repeating numbers and even non-repeating numbers to get your attention. Some of the most seen numbers are these below— each number has a special meaning from the archangels.

Here are some of the meanings:

111: Make a wish, the angels are here to make your dreams a reality for your highest good.

222: Have faith and keep your vibration high to continue the connection with your spiritual team.

333: The angels want you to know Jesus and many master teachers are here with you.

444: The angels are surrounding you with love and guidance.

911: Pay attention to your thoughts, keep them positive, and notice what is happening around you in the moment you see this number.

944: Take responsibility for your life choices, clean up your energetic space, and make your life mission a priority.

144: Keep moving forward, and don't let others tell you that you can't do it. This is a miraculous time to receive answers and solutions as you need them.

When you do receive the gift of these angelic signs, I encourage you to share a prayer of gratitude each time. This will enhance your connection with the archangels.

Dress intentionally and connect to your archangels with ease

Archangel Jophiel and Archangel Chamuel are the two main archangels who supported me when I was searching for more spiritual meaning in my life, and helped me feel the joy of getting dressed each day. These angels helped me to embrace my body and the lifestyle that I have been given, and have helped me to realize what a gift it is to be alive. I find myself excited to wake up each morning feeling the energy of the archangels and their readiness to connect with me through the colors of my clothes. Are you ready to dress intentionally so you can connect to your archangels with ease? I am so excited to teach, guide and support women with connecting to the archangels, while having fun with colors and offering intuitive messages that motivate them to enjoy life. Think about how you can invite the archangels into your life, and how they will enhance your joy, increase your self-love, and show you your personal strength, while seeing the beauty of the world! Remember to always ask for, believe in, and be open to receive the archangels' love and light. I am so grateful to share the five angels above with you, and hope that you will always know that you are loved by all the angels. And so it is.

CHAPTER

Eight

Quit: How Science And Angels Can Transform Your Life
By Donna Kiel

DONNA KIEL

Donna Kiel has dedicated her life to helping others achieve their highest and truest potential, and find passion and purpose in life. As a counselor, teacher, principal, life coach, and mentor, Donna has inspired thousands in gaining self-awareness and achieving greater levels of personal and professional success. She holds three degrees, including a BA in psychology, an MA in counseling, and a doctorate in leadership. Donna's approach provides a practical method of self-assessment that can be applied every day to confidently live a life of meaningful purpose. Donna's specialties include compassionate leadership, innovative organizational change, team building, personal transformation, loss and crisis resolution, and mediation. Donna works with individuals and groups through her services as a mentor, coach, workshop leader, and consultant. Donna offers free assessment and consultation for those seeking growth. She can be reached at drdonnakiel@gmail.com or through her website at www.donnakiel.com.

Acknowledgments

In all our lives, there are times when we stumble, fall, and lose our way. It is the compassion of others that lifts our soul and brings new light. My deepest gratitude to those in my life who have forgiven my imperfection, who have seen in me that which I could not, and who have given me the inspiration that became my words on the page. To my family, friends, colleagues, clients, and students, I thank you for sharing your hearts with me. To my greatest muse, my granddaughter, Charlotte Sue, your life gave my life new meaning and purpose, and with one smile, I found fearless love and the courage to speak my truth. I owe the deepest gratitude to my imperfection, fear, sorrow, and loss. Within each moment of suffering, I have found the greatest of teachers and the truth of mercy.

Quit: How Science And Angels Can Transform Your Life
By Donna Kiel

"The one you are looking for is the one who is looking." — Francis of Assisi

What are you afraid of? I'm afraid fear will get in the way of fully living my life. For me, fear has been the soundtrack of my life, either playing in the background or at times loudly blasting. Within fear are messages, both scientific and angelically spiritual, that can lead us to unlock our truest self and transform our lives.

My earliest memory is being afraid. I was afraid of being alone, being lost, being powerless—I was simply afraid. As an introverted middle child of a complex family, I grew up in an environment where we pretended to be normal, like those perfect families on TV. My family's superpower was pretending that we were not afraid and that everything was fine. Over time, pretending became natural.

Fearful families tend to fight—a lot. Desperately afraid of conflict, I became a peace-seeking people-pleaser. My way of making everyone happy was to use my intelligence and curiosity to create my indispensable position in the family as "the fixer." Becoming a fixer had its benefits. My people-pleasing fixing paved the way for me to become a counselor, teacher, and school principal.

Raised Catholic, my family's rituals during a crisis, consisted of reciting rosaries and invoking the saints to keep disaster away. Despite my faith, I was silently skeptical of the magic of votive candles and statues of saints. Early in my life, I began searching to find a more practical, reliable, and scientific approach than prayer to avoid suffering. I thought if my family was pretending that we were doing fine, they were also pretending that prayer and angels worked. I looked to science, psychology, and self-help for solutions, but would keep that Hail Mary handy—in case some angels and saints had my back after all.

Both science and spirituality confirm there is a power greater than our mind at work in our lives. Whether that power is an angel or simply exists in the laws of physics (or both) is a matter of perspective. For me, science and angels merged when my fears could no longer be contained by pretending I was fine.

The feeling of fear can be a wonderful catalyst for transformation. The journey begins when we attempt to manage our fear.

Fear motivated my searching for an angel or a strategy that would calm the anxiousness that caused my suffering. As is true for most enlightenment, it was in the depth of despair, that I realized I was looking for the wrong solution. I had wanted some winged being to save me, or a scientific approach, but it was within deep suffering that I discovered that "angel" is a way of living supported by scientific research.

At the moment that we pivot our minds and hearts to deeply know that there is more to every experience than what we see on the surface, we open our hearts to the truth. For me, the realization was that "angel" is a process—a way of living.

When we "accept notice of the gracious enlightenment in living" (A.N.G.E.L.), we remove the blinders that otherwise distort our soul's truth. In what follows, I describe how the ANGEL practice emerged in my life and how you can use it to transform your life fearlessly.

Where Science and Angelic Spirituality Merge

As I researched methods to ease suffering, I discovered the simple teaching of the splendor of recognition emerging from eastern spirituality. The teaching states that God, or the divine, has hidden a part of itself within each of us. The teaching states that this was done to help us spend our lives recognizing that splendor in ourselves and others.

Interestingly, Sigmund Freud's theory of projection and Carl Jung's notion of "the shadow" align with the spiritual teachings of splendor of recognition. Both the idea of projection and theories about the shadow suggest that what we dislike in ourselves is what we tend to dislike in others, and what we see as our beauty and strength is what we esteem in others.

Spirituality and psychology also intersect with Newton's third law of motion, which holds that for every action, there is an equal and opposite reaction. What we put out into the world is what comes back to us.

The realization that the intelligence, beauty, and wisdom I saw in others was also in me, shifted my worldview. I also realized that what I despised in others was also in me. Beauty and ugliness dwell in each of us, and knowing this truth gives us the power to transform. The splendor of recognition, projection, the shadow, and the third law of motion are the foundation from which living the practice of ANGEL is apparent and actionable. I have found the angel practice can be lived through three steps.

Accepting Notice

Step one is to accept notice that something must change. Often, we fight against changing our beliefs and expectations of how life *should* be. Change tends to breed fear. But, to grow, you must accept notice that fear is an invitation to transform. The moment you feel your body tense, uptightness in your chest, a lump in your throat, the pounding of your heart, or the sweat on your palms—it is time to take notice and to take action. Living with and leaning into fear is one of life's greatest challenges. It is a challenge I have struggled with for as long as I remember.

I was raised in the '60s and '70s as a proud peace-loving, moccasin-wearing, self-righteous woman determined to make the world a better place, and I was fearfully living a lie that began when I was six.

My brother Roger was born with Down Syndrome when I was six, and my parents decided to place him in an institution. Although it was common at the time (1965), my parents never talked much about their decision or their reasons. And I never asked.

A caregiver for my brother gave my mother the book "Angel Unaware." The book describes Down Syndrome children as angels among us. Seeing Roger as an angel was my mother's antidote to her fear, but was confusion for me. Roger's life brought me a complex dichotomy of love, loss, and fear. I not only lost the image of a brother, but I also lost who I was supposed to be. Society told me Roger was inferior and deficient, and my love for him became an inner conflict.

Every weekend we would visit Roger in the institution, and occasionally, we would bring him home—only to take him back. Amid that confusing ritual, I became a silent observer of life rather than a participant. I searched to know how never to be given away. I reasoned, "If an angel isn't good enough to live here, how could I ever be good enough?" I needed to do more, achieve more, be more so that I would not be given away.

Fear and confusion were a constant as I grew up with Roger. I kept fear at bay by distracting myself with working hard. I also worked hard to keep an emotional distance from Roger.

My mother died in 2003 when Roger was 38. After her death, I became Roger's guardian.

At the time, I was a successful school principal and completing my doctorate. I had made a busy life for myself. Against that background, becoming Roger's guardian was an interruption. I was too busy even to realize I was afraid of what guardianship would mean in my life.

I made excuses for not bringing Roger to my family's home for visits. I spewed self-righteous anger at society's treatment of people with disabilities and pretended things were fine. In truth, my new role in Roger's life was a flashing neon sign of notice that my soul was appalled by the lie I was living.

If we are lucky, our lives reach a point when our soul says "enough." If we ignore the notice, life will kick us in the gut. For me, that kick happened when Roger's caretaker called saying he had cancer. My brother was not going to allow me to continue living the lie that I was not good enough to be loved, or to continue living the lie that I did not love him.

Accepting Notice Strategy

Through suffering, we are given notice of what we need to accept to work through our fear. Accepting notice and allowing suffering is the greatest expression of self-compassion required for transformation.

To use the angel process in your life, here are some questions to ask yourself:

- What am I avoiding in my life right now?
- What is life whispering to me right now?
- What fear, judgment, and resistance am I experiencing?

As you begin to answer these questions, notices will appear. Take notice and move to the next step.

Gracious Enlightenment

Step two is the process of gracious enlightenment. It involves freeing ourselves from fear by seeking answers to our life's questions. To become graciously enlightened is to compassionately release the fears and lies we tell ourselves in our attempt to believe we are protected from change and that we are in control.

I had been lying to myself that I didn't love and need Roger because he was Down Syndrome and I was "normal." I felt far from normal. It had been easier not to love the intellectually limited brother who would be shipped away each week. Given my self-imposed detachment from him, dealing with his cancer would merely be another job.

Roger's cancer required radiation and treatment. I scheduled things in my life to flex with Roger's appointments. I brought work and reading along with me so that I didn't waste "valuable time." Amidst these distractions, I didn't expect Roger's pain and suffering to become mine. With each cry, he turned to me and yelled my name. His eyes were filled with panic and fear, and my heart broke into a million pieces. Roger's pain became my pain, and I found and used the words that he could not to calm him. Now, the fear I had always carried (of loving my brother) had no room in my soul. I let go of the idea of a "normal" sibling relationship and opened my heart to *our* relationship.

During radiation treatments, I calmed Roger by holding his small hand. I studied his pinky fingers and their inward curve, and thought back to his first step as an infant as he held my hand. Now, he was holding me and giving me support.

To distract him, I played his favorite movie, *The Wizard of Oz*. While we sat together, staring at the screen, I felt myself release the fearful lie that I was the one who was defective and ugly. I released the lie that I was displeasing God because I was so angry at him for Roger, and the biggest lie—that I would not be lost without my brother—of course I would be lost. I let go of the self-hatred I harbored for not loving Roger enough. Gracious enlightenment and powerful love of my baby brother washed over me, and love replaced fear.

Fear and love cannot exist in the same place, and allowing love of myself and Roger created the compassion we both needed.

Gracious Enlightenment Strategy

Gracious enlightenment occurs when we allow ourselves to release the lies that prevent us from seeing our beauty and the beauty in others. In moving towards gracious enlightenment, I encourage you to ask yourself the questions:

- What am I doing strictly to be accepted or liked?
- What part of what I am doing do I need to release?
- What lies am I telling myself that I need to give up?

Enlightenment involves releasing an image of what we think our lives *should* be, and welcoming our truth.

Living

Step three is to live with a clear vision of what you want. Life is what happens while we are trying to figure out what we want. Each moment of life brings us messages to become clear on what we want, value, believe, and hope for. Our job is to listen to these messages and to decode them so that we can clearly articulate, for ourselves and our soul, what it is we want in life.

For this, we need to be specific.

The problem is that most of us are experts in making vague generalities, like: "I want a happy life," and "I want to be successful." To fully let go of lies, we need to state—simply, clearly, and unwaveringly—what we want. It was fearless love that allowed me to open my heart to welcome the specificity of what I want in life.

My brother died on a Monday at 11:00 p.m., four months before his 40th birthday. At his funeral, after I delivered a controlled, articulate, and deeply moving eulogy, the priest surprised everyone as he sang a beautiful a cappella version of "Somewhere Over the Rainbow." As he sang, I could picture my hand on Roger's in that hospital room only weeks before. I tried desperately to stop the tears that were becoming the ugly cry.

Although he was mostly non-verbal, Roger had a few phrases he would repeat. His favorite phrase was "I quit." He would loudly say, "I quit," and then laugh hysterically. As the priest sang, I could hear him saying, "I quit," and feel his laughter in my heart.

His simple phrase permitted me to quit running, to quit pretending. I gave myself permission to quit searching outside myself, to quit judging, blaming, and believing the lie that I was not enough. I gave myself permission to love myself and love my brother—exactly as we are.

At Roger's funeral, I prayed that I could find the words to inspire myself and others so that fear will not control our lives. The specificity of that prayer—the words that surfaced from deep within—became the transformation of my life, from the overworked school principal to a professor, life coach, and writer. My life is still filled with fear, but knowing I have permission to quit pretending that I can love the messy, imperfectly perfect angel-self was Roger's most loving gift.

Living Strategy

The greatest gift we can give ourselves is to state what we want clearly. The following questions can help you to get clear:

- Where in your life do you need permission to quit?
- What is it that you need to laugh about after you quit?

You are the angel the world is waiting for, and you have permission to quit searching, pretending, and fighting against the fear so that you, too, can have fearless truth and love.

CHAPTER

Nine

Saving A Place For Mickey
By Elizabeth Harbin

ELIZABETH HARBIN

Elizabeth is a psychic medium, Reiki Master, hypnosis practitioner, radio show host, professional card reader, minister, and the best-selling author of the books, *Healer* and *Inspirations*. She eagerly changed careers in 1999 from the corporate world into metaphysics, where she continues her private practice in North Texas and abroad. Her metaphysical classes and events are a great source of information for those starting out on their metaphysical journey. To get in touch with Elizabeth, text her at 214-454-0072, or go to

her Facebook page at
https://www.facebook.com/elizabethharbinpsychic.

Acknowledgments

A special thank you must go to Kyra and Todd Schaefer of As You Wish Publishing for their assistance, guidance, and love in assisting me in making this chapter come to fruition. My tribe, for their love and support. My family and of course, my mother, who is constantly opening doors for me from the other side. Last but not least, the Archangel Michael for his numerous interventions, guidance, and of course, protection.

Saving A Place For Mickey
By Elizabeth Harbin

Growing up, I was fortunate in the fact that my mom was open-minded about metaphysics. Of course, she would be—I chose her, right? She knew all about palmistry, tarot cards, past life regressions, automatic writing, and so much more. Her biggest love was astrology, and because she reveled in it, I knew all about my sign, her sign, my brother's sign—well, you get the picture. I loved being that innocent Piscean child, and having my detailed and knowledgeable Aquarian mom explain all the mysteries of all the houses, planets, compatibility, and of course, famous people that shared my birth date! As I grew older, my interests and curiosity about metaphysics continued, but not at the same pace or importance as earning a living and finding my life's pathway.

By my mid-40s, I realized that my path was not that of the corporate world, and I began to take steps towards the path of metaphysics. I loved to go to fairs to get readings from various psychics, palmists, and card readers. Eventually, I met my mentor Samantha Lawrence Key, and I learned how to read Old Gypsy Fortune Telling Cards. After that, I took as many metaphysical classes as I could afford, and yet, I still felt like my life's pathway eluded me. Something was missing.

Then came the summer encounter that would eventually change my life forever. My mom, brother, and I were born in Alabama, but in 1969, we moved to the Lone Star State.

She took us in and convinced us that this is where we would put down new roots and forever call Texas our home. Did you go to family reunions when you were growing up? We did. Back in the '80s and '90s, our small band of wild Texans would pack up my brother's van, and we would hit the road to the beautiful, white, sandy beaches of Gulf Shores, Alabama. Our relatives were scattered all over the U.S., but the majority of them lived in the heart of Dixie, and because there were so many of us, we had to plan our reunions a year in advance.

Our small family of three took various different paths during that time—divorce, marriage, kids, and numerous jobs. We all tried to get back to our roots often, but during the early years, it was a struggle, and busy lives were always the culprit. Finally, in the late '90s, we started making plans to unite the various tribes, and Gulf Shores became our destination. During this reunion, our families overtook the Condos of Gulf Shores. There were so many of us there, the management actually put a welcome sign on their marquee out in their front reception area. There was never a time when we did not run into a cousin or four on the elevators! Most of the time, everyone was on their own. You'd either go to the beach, deep-sea fishing, golf, or relax on comfy chaise lounges on your balconies, while watching the surf ebb and flow as the world went by. We had several dinners planned for this reunion so that we could all gather and see everyone at one time. During one of these family dinners, a cousin of mine and I were talking about the children and our parents and, of course, the other cousins, and how we all had enjoyed such great childhoods together. She remembered things that frankly blew my mind, and with her amazing ability to remember details, I was clearly her captive audience! Then, like a bolt out of the blue, she looked me right in the eyes and asked, "Do you remember your imaginary friend Mickey? And do you remember how you always had to save a place for him? Yeah, you even had your mother set a place for him at the dinner table!" I simply stood there. Nothing registered. How could I have forgotten such an important part of my life? Who the heck was Mickey, and what had happened to him? Why did he leave? Was she sure that I was the one with this imaginary friend? Little did I know that the answer to these questions and more would be revealed several years later.

I would never forget that reunion. Somehow it set in motion my need to find out the answers of my mysterious invisible friend. My mom did confirm that I had an imaginary friend named Mickey, but with no more information than I got at the reunion. Eventually, I put that trip back into my memories file, and my life decided to take a drastic turn. I moved to Houston. I loved living there and living in such a diverse city. Metaphysical stores were everywhere, and most of them close to where I lived!

A few of the people I worked with loved metaphysical shops as much as I did, and we eventually came upon the shop that would give me more information than any other shop since. This amazing place was full of crystals, books, drums, jewelry, gifted psychics, and intuitive masters! One particular evening I brought a friend from work to this goldmine, and while we were perusing the books and eyeing their jewelry and crystals, one of the psychics came up to us and asked if we would like to try a past life regression. It would only be a sample, but with enough information to give us a taste of what a regression was like. Oh my God! How could I pass this up? The psychic led me to what looked like a massage table and I was told to lie on my back. She positioned herself behind my head and placed her hands forward toward my toes. Her hands became stationary above my heart chakra, and she began to tell me about one of my past lives from the Aztec period. Apparently, I was one of the people who performed the sacrifices of the chosen few for the assurance of good and prosperous crops. Then she picked up the time period where I lived as an Incan priest. All of this was interesting and, yes, a little disturbing, but then she asked, "You want to know who Mickey was?" You could have knocked me off that table! How in this world could she possibly have known about Mickey? All I could do was nod my head, yes. I could feel my ears straining to hear every single word she was about to say. It turns out that Mickey was the Archangel Michael and that, as a child, I had called him Mickey. Then the biggest shock of all came. She asked if I knew that the Archangel Michael had intervened twice on my behalf when I was a kid, somewhere between the ages of six and eight. Yes! I remembered! Once, when I was around six or seven years old, I was riding my bike to show my mom and dad how good I had gotten riding down the small hill across from our house. Long story short, I came riding downhill, turned right, and all I saw ahead of me was headlights. The next thing I remembered was being in a ditch, still on my bike, and not one scratch on me! That memory flooded my mind as I lay on that table. Then, I remembered the time I was playing with a rope on a tree. The rope got caught around my neck, and I could not reach the ground with my toes! Not sure how that was resolved either, but I do remember I felt as if someone had lifted me up the tree to get the rope untangled, and that I had a rope burn around my neck. Again, my parents were horrified. What they must have thought of me at that time!

My time on the psychic's table was coming to an end, and she stopped for a few seconds, I guess to let my emotions get back in check. She then continued, saying that at some point, a father figure had told me that Mickey was not real, and soon after that, Mickey disappeared. Immediately, I knew who that person had been—my grandfather. He had told me that my imaginary friend Mickey was not real and that I needed to grow up. What? Then the psychic asked if I knew that my grandfather had meant well. Did he mean well? Seriously? Again she spoke in soft tones and said, "You have a purpose on this earth, and one day you will discover what that purpose is. Just know that it will happen." Suddenly she stopped. The reading was over. A million questions came pouring in, but I knew I had to leave. As I made my way back to the front counter, one of the owners happened to be there. "Apparently, she gave you some of the answers to your questions," he said. Words escaped me, and again, all I could do was nod my head, yes. He chuckled, and my friend and I left the building. I pondered about how my life might have been so different had that event with my grandfather never taken place. For a time, I was extremely angry about it. Eventually, I realized that I had to get over that kind of anger, and be glad about having been reminded of my amazing encounter with Mickey, even if it did take over 40 years!

Several months after that amazing reading, I decided that the corporate rat race world was not my calling and that my time in Houston was up. Could it be that I moved to Houston solely to experience that reading? At that time, I had no clue, but what I did know for sure was that it was time for me to move on. I could feel that my missing piece had been found. So, I packed up and moved back to the Dallas-Ft. Worth area. Yes, I was going home.

It's now 25 years later. My working in corporate is a blur, and I am now a psychic medium, author, hypnosis practitioner, ordained minister, radio show host, and teacher of metaphysics. Archangel Michael and I have developed a rather close relationship now. He is always the first one to show up if my clients need him, or if he wants me to know that he has done an intervention on their behalf. It is amazing how my clients get what I am talking about when it comes to Michael. They recognize the information and will usually tell me their Michael stories! For those of you who have not had an encounter with this amazing Archangel, here are a few items I would like to share with you. Archangel Michael's name means "Who is like the Divine" or "Who is like God." His main purpose is to protect God's children in every way, as well as to give clarity and courage. He is the defender of truth and the righter of wrongs. He is associated with the Sun. The essential oils that represent him are frankincense and orange. What colors are linked to him? Violet, gold, and blue. When I see his presence, it's always in a blue or white orb. The symbols for him are the sword of light and the shield of truth.

At times, the Archangel Michael can make his presence known by you being able to hear his voice loud and clear. I have only had one experience in that. It was a time before I knew all about him, and I was at a job interview. The company where I had worked for over 20 years was downsizing due to a takeover. I did not want to leave, but I had to at least go to this interview to make corporate happy. While in the interview, the lady said to me, "Now you know that if you accept this job, you will never be able to go back home?" What a thing to say, right? Well, it's all I could hear. I left the interview with a decline on the job offer, returned to the office, and learned that one of my dearest friends had announced her retirement that day, and that I had a new job to apply for in the location I loved. Yes, I got the job. Was The Voice that kept repeating in my mind about not being able to go back home, Michael? Yes, I truly believe it was. Mainly, because I have not had another experience so vocal and so loud again in my life.

So what else can I tell you about the Archangel Michael? His day is believed to be Sunday. There are way too many crystals to list for him, so I always go with the colors that I feel represent him. Lapis for blue. Amethyst for purple. Gold jewelry of any kind. Last, but not least, is the belief that Michael is the sponsor of police departments and law enforcement agencies around the world. So, if you want to purchase gifts for your favorite police officer, or items of protection for you or a loved one, go on a new adventure and visit a Catholic store. There will be so much to look at with the medallions and necklaces and prayers they have for all saints, not only Michael. I keep several Archangel Michael medallions in my pocket and purse as well as in my home and auto.

In closing this chapter, I would like to leave you with a prayer I say every day. May this bless you and keep you protected in all ways!

Archangel Michael, please place a protective bubble of white light around me. Do not let other energies affect me or my divine purpose. Please use your sword of light to cut any cords or ties to anything and anyone who has been or will try to do so in my future from holding me back. Please shower white light healing energies over me and use your shield of truth to protect me always and forever. Amen and blessed be!

Update. Before finishing this chapter, I became extremely ill. A UTI infection became a kidney infection, with a fast track to going sepsis. While in the hospital, I was visited by what looked like death. A large, black crow with a golden head walked in front of my hospital bed, and with a sneer and a hissing sound, walked right through my door. It was not until I had returned home and had a chance to rethink this event that I realized that during that night, my friend had put all of my crystals and my Archangel Michael medallions in a blue see-through bag, and that she had placed the bag next to my right hand. Did the Archangel Michael intervene for me yet again? I will never be convinced otherwise!

CHAPTER

Ten

From Worlds Of Light To Worlds Of Multidimensionality
By Genevieve Ivey

GENEVIVE IVEY

Genevieve Ivey is an energy intuitive, bodyworker, teacher, and workshop facilitator of soul embodiment and self-mastery. She has assisted thousands of people in self-transformation and healing. She is certified in many healing modalities, but prefers the journey of Soul Embodiment, in which one allows the purest and most powerful essence of all that they are, to fully anchor in every moment. Her heart's song is assisting others on the journey of remembering, trusting, and surrendering to who they truly are. You can learn more at SoultoSoul.love or contact Genevieve for information on offerings at puresoulpresence@gmail.com.

Acknowledgments

To my love, Trevi, and my greatest teachers, Christian, Leia, Sofie, Luke, and Navi—you are the stars in my sky, my constellation, none shine more brightly than you.

From Worlds Of Light
To Worlds Of Multidimensionality
By Genevieve Ivey

Faeries. I work with faeries, or *fae*. Integrating the world of the *fae* as part of my truth took almost ten years. So, the session when a being of great presence and love came in for a client, was a day I began to remember what it looks like to walk the path of a healer. The room felt full of an energy unfamiliar to me. It was a palpable presence, strong, familiar yet forgotten, an undeniable presence of love. I intuited that it was an angel. At that moment I realized my determination to hold fast to what I thought I knew, had in fact, kept me trapped in a world of denial with limiting beliefs of what I thought it must look like to be a mother, a healer, and person who walks on this earth.

The moment the angel came into my session began my awakening—an awakening that continues with each day. I remembered that the healer's path is a never-ending journey of letting go and allowing; a journey of constant healing and growth. As I walk this path toward my individual sovereignty and pure presence, I am also able to assist others in their spiritual growth. This includes the remembrance of how to anchor their authentic soul self.

During my awakening, I have gone through a series of self-initiations; a remembering of who I am and what gifts I bring with me to the planet to help my brothers and sisters. For years, I would wake up in the middle of the night with energy and light pouring through my body. I noticed others I couldn't see in the room helping me as I embodied and assimilated what felt like massive amounts of energy. I remembered that this energy was only me, all the parts of me that I asked to be here as one at this time in the world.

Over the past twenty years, I have painstakingly grown into my role as a soul mother and healer. I am a mother to many souls as they remember and embody who they are and how to come back into alignment with the song of their soul. This can also include embodying different parts of their body's consciousness, as well as disconnected or misplaced energetic bodies. I am also the mother of five beautiful children whose soul work is also of major importance to the planet. I tend to them gently and support the soul maintenance required for self-awareness to blossom and grow.

Trusting Your Team

I can see color in and around the body. Energies that are dark and lifeless or energies that are vibrating with colors that are rarely seen except in bioluminescent creatures found in nature. Faeries can easily work to change these bodies of light and bring them into balance with nature so they can heal. I wasn't sure how angels fit into my body of work, or how I felt about working with them. At the time, these teams did not like to work together. When one came forward, the other would depart. And so began my journey of merging the angelic world and the world of fae. There was an entire matrix that was created to bridge worlds during healing sessions. Working with faeries in a world of color and light is extremely different from the worlds and energies of the angelic realm. I had to learn to trust these powerful energies and the shifts that can unfold during and after a session. Today I work with both faeries and angels. There is a magic that happens between these worlds to open awareness and expansion within the human experience, making room for shifts in consciousness, while healing trauma and wounds in the body.

Working with the angelic realm is such a beautiful and rewarding experience. However, doubt and fear can keep you from fully stepping into this role. You can step onto your path with the angels with grace and joy by being diligent and working through what stands between you and the angelic realms. Remember to keep moving forward with love, find your highest light, and let it shine!

Over the years, my sessions have become purely channeled from the angelic realm, the realm of the ancient ones known as fae, as well as guides and even galactic teams when available. These teams work together to assist us, just as they are currently working together to help Gaia during this time of change and transformation.

Ways to Work with Your Angelic Team

Let go of the idea that you know what it means to work with angels. Allow them to show you. Angels don't truly have names, they have songs, harmonies, frequencies, vibrations, waves, pulses—a language within a language of expansive tones. The way that translates from healer to healer or communicator to communicator is vastly different, so, there is plenty of room for your experience and the way you hear, see, feel, or know angels. Learning to listen with all your senses helps deepen your awareness of their presence in your life. They love to communicate with synchronicities. Synchronicity is a language of information and manifestation that creates an alignment which unfolds perfectly before your eyes.

Sometimes when I'm out running errands, throughout the day, I will notice the same person everywhere I go. I see them at the grocery store, then I drive across town to UPS, and the same person that caught my eye is there. Later at dinner with a friend, I notice the same person at the table beside me. For me, this is a message from spirit that says, "We are always with you. Be still and know there is a bigger plan and you are on the right path. Thank you." I always feel joyful and emotional knowing I am seen and loved. What beautiful synchronicities are in your life? These create a map for you to stay on your soul path, as well as a reminder that the angels are always with you and available. Ask them to work with you and then follow the synchronicities!

Synchronicities with Numbers

Archangels Ariel and Uriel would like to activate angelic codes of light with you! Take a deep breath and receive the transmission of the codes of light that are available to you now.

Angel numbers are numbers that the angels may be using to communicate with you. When you see the same number sequence everywhere you turn, you can be pretty sure this is information the angels are sharing with you.

These angelic light codes can be used to activate parts of yourself that you've forgotten, placed aside, or haven't yet embodied. For instance, when you see the number sequence 1111 consistently, try calling on Archangels Ariel and Uriel to activate the angelic code with you. To give this experience a try, tap into your knowing and creative nature to allow the perfect words to come forward for you. As an example, you might say, "I ask Archangels Ariel and Uriel (or my angelic team) to activate the angelic light code of 1111 in my body of light and all my cells." Allow yourself to receive the activation and feel the energetic shifts in your body. Then notice what's different for you in your life, in your interactions with others, and in your body. With the light code 1111, you might feel more connected to your power or things might begin to change rapidly for you. Light is information, and there is an infinite amount of light you can learn from all around us in every moment.

Harmonics—A Gift from the Angelic Realm

Archangels Metatron, Chamuel, and Azrael would like to share the gift of harmonics with you. Harmonics is an angelic healing tool that can smooth out energies, situations, and emotions. Mastery of the heart is necessary to master harmonics, as the energy comes from another dimension, which is accessible through the heart space. Chamuel can help you with this gift of love and presence. Breath work requires using the breath to create deep awareness within yourself. Use the breath to bring your consciousness and full awareness into your heart. Allow your breath to flow in and out of your heart, as you intentionally breathe into this space. Work with Chamuel as you master your heart breathing. Simply ask Archangel Chamuel to breathe with you into your heart and feel it open and expand with every breath. Allow him to show you the many worlds that exist within this space, as you explore what it means to heart breathe and open the door to the love you have to offer the world.

Archangel Azrael can help you bring the glory of love into the darkest place within your heart. If you find yourself lost within, call on Azrael to shine his light during any moments that keep you from being in your joy. He is a master of joy and love in moments of hopelessness, fear, loss, and grief. The heart itself is limitless, and the energies and the worlds it connects us to are also limitless. Your heart is a healing tool that you can learn to master in every moment and every interaction of your being-ness! And in every moment your breath can be heart-centered and loving. Challenge yourself to stay here, and everything will change for you.

Harmonics can be used for great healing for yourself and others. There are countless ways to use harmonics. Harmonics is a tone of very high frequency that can be called forward to change energy and the way it interacts, feels, and exists in the world. One way you can work with harmonics is to take an object that is heavy when it should feel light because it is impregnated with energy, or maybe it lost its glow or luster. Hold the object in your hands. Connect with the object with your heart. Feel the spirit of the object (how wonderful is it that everything has spirit?). How does it feel? What is it telling you? Now, intend to run the energy of the object. Remember to stay connected with your heart, and this is your point of power during the work. Your power keeps you anchored in the *now*. Feel the energy of the object intensify. Once you do intend to run harmonics through the object, take a deep breath into your heart that says, "I am." Feel the energy of the object intensify and begin to shift. Breathe again and feel deeply into your heart and the object.

Now release with a gentle sigh or exhale. How has the object changed? What do you notice?

Have fun with the angelic energy of harmonics as it can be used for anything. And remember, everything has an individual song! Listen with your heart and learn to hear your beautiful and unique song.

Your Angelic Team of Light

My team consists of many angels. I have remembered deep love for Archangel Zachriel, Archangel Orion, Archangel Metatron, Archangel Azrael, Archangel Magdalene, and Archangel Gabriel. My angelic team is always changing and expanding. I have worked with each one on various projects for extended periods. During the co-creation of angelic Sekhem-Seichim, a healing modality about remembering and anchoring your healing gifts, my angelic team was constantly by my side, giving me information and helping me remember.

During this time, while in REM-sleep, an angel came to me. She radiated beauty, wisdom, and love, and was in human form. She seemed to have a golden glow that emanated from her very presence. There was a knowing that passed between us. I knew who she was by her smile, which answered every question I could have ever asked. There was no need for words. And then her face changed into a blank form. It was as if she had no face, but she was still beautiful. She nodded towards a table. At the table sat people I have had interactions with throughout my life, such as friends, colleagues, and others which whom I had worked with on various odd jobs. It was understood that she could be anyone. I woke up knowing I had one of the most profound interactions of life. I was in communion with one of the angels that I work with and have worked with in multiple moments my entire life.

The dream state is the perfect time to communicate with angels. Raise your vibration before bed, set the intention, and ask your angels for healing as you sleep, or ask for help with a problem you are currently experiencing in life. As you enter the different states of brain waves with your vibration in an altered state, you can easily enter the angelic realm, and interaction with your angels is possible!

Healing with Archangel Zachriel

My first interaction with Zachriel was during a moment of great suffering and sadness for me. I felt as if I couldn't stand another second of cruelty from the world. I felt him as I prayed for help. I asked who he was, and he told me he was Zachriel. I asked how he could help me, and he showed me a memory—one that didn't haunt me, but that was unpleasant. As my mind recalled the memory, my body's response to it began to lessen more and more until I felt neutral about the memory altogether. Then I felt nothing but relief.

We worked together throughout the day as he worked on healing traumatic memories I was holding on to. Within a few hours, I felt happier and stronger. He is one of my favorite angels to work with, and I'm grateful beyond measure for his gifts of healing. Beyond being open and aware, try to practice the art of staying in the question and always allow yourself to be shown what an experience can be without expectation.

Miracles are all around you and happening to you all the time. You must have the eyes to see. Ask your angelic team to help you shift your perspective. For instance, if there is a tense moment at home or at work, you can simply say to your angelic team or the angel you are currently working with, "Show me how to shine my light in this moment," or "Show me how to bring joy into this moment." Before you know it, the inspiration will come to you, and along with it your light and joy!

My angelic realization has assisted my personal growth and remembering—remembering the magnificence of the body as a vessel for the soul, remembering why I am here and the gifts I bring, remembering the wisdom and know-ledge I bring and to always stay connected to my knowing and truth. There is a code of angelic healing that can be unlocked in each of us. When we are ready, they assist us in our expansion of consciousness, our expansion of self, and our connection to life.

CHAPTER

Eleven

She Talks To Angels
By Brandi Khan

BRANDI KHAN

In addition to homeschooling her four children, Brandi Khan works as a certified Angel Therapy Practitioner, an intuitive medium, and a Reiki Master. After receiving a life-changing message from spirit regarding a family member, Brandi decided to devote her life to delivering messages to those in need. She has been a featured guest on Hay House radio with her mentor, James Van Praagh. Brandi also works as a member of the talented psychic medium group, "The Houston Trio." She also channels healing energy from the Arcturians, who are one of the most advanced civilizations in the galaxy. Brandi lives in Lake Jackson, Texas with her husband, four children, and two dogs. To learn more about the services that Brandi offers, please visit: www.BrandiKhan.com.

Acknowledgments

First and foremost, I want to thank my guardian angel for being my inspiration. And to my spirit team that always backs me up—thank you! To my mother, Gale Walker, J.D., thank you for your invaluable help and support with the writing process. Having your love and support means so much to me. To my father, (Booker Walker 1949-2016), thank you for listening to my experiences with angels and the spirit world. You always believed me. And for that, I am forever grateful. To my husband Afzal, you make it possible for me to pursue all of my dreams. Thank you for always being there for me. I couldn't do this without you. Thank you to my children, Amir, Amirah, Ali, and Aydin, for being so proud to call me your mother. To Brooke, Bev, and Brian, thank you for making this journey called life so much fun.

She Talks To Angels
By Brandi Khan

I was six years old when I decided to form a club with neighborhood friends. Since I had quite a fascination with anything dealing with angels, I named our group the "Free Angels." I even used my mom's typewriter to draft a code of conduct for the members of the club. Pretty strange for a young girl, right? I was always a little different, and I knew that I didn't quite fit in with other kids my age. I remember meticulously cleaning my bedroom one day, and then placing three small chairs in the middle of the room. The chairs were for angels, whom I invited to sit and watch me while I sang and danced for them. Feeling their love, support, and adoration was a joy. I never doubted their existence.

As a teenager, I disconnected from my ability to interact with angels when I accepted religious teachings that discouraged contact with the spirit world. I was taught that it was harmful. Those were lonely years for me. I felt incomplete, as if a part of me was missing.

Twenty-five years later, I felt compelled to reconnect with my angels again. So one morning, I asked for a sign. As I looked out of the upstairs window in our family study, I implored, "Guardian angel, I feel you all around me, but I need a sign from you. Please let me know that I am not alone." Five minutes later, I went downstairs. As I walked into the kitchen, I looked up and saw a delicate, white feather slowly drifting down through the air. I gasped and extended my hand, allowing the feather to land in my palm. My request had been answered! Profoundly grateful, I thanked my guardian angel. In that auspicious moment, my life changed. I knew that I wanted to teach others about the wonderful world of angels.

Guardian Angels

Many of the world's great religions—including Christianity, Judaism, and Islam—recognize that an angel is divinely assigned to each person at birth. Angels are aware of our thoughts, intentions, and emotions. They always hold us in a space of love and compassion, even when we make mistakes. Angels have a higher vision for our lives, and they will lovingly inspire us to reach our fullest potential. In times of difficulty, our guardian angels will surround us with figurative wings of comfort and support.

Neither male nor female, angels are divine beings who have never experienced a human incarnation. However, in dire situations, guardian angels can appear in human form when they need to intervene or to deliver messages. They desire for you to make decisions in accordance with your higher self, but they will never interfere with your free will. Angels are unconditionally loving beings in action.

Children are naturally open to the angelic kingdom because of their innocence. They are able to see, hear, and feel on a deep level because they have not lost their ability to believe in the supernatural. Consequently, it is common for young children to speak about their encounters with angels.

My son, Ali, had an experience with his guardian angel during our family vacation in San Juan, Puerto Rico. As we walked back to our hotel one afternoon, we spotted a deserted area along an otherwise crowded beach. We strolled along the shore, enjoying the breathtaking scenery. My husband pointed to a rocky outcrop that offered a fantastic view of the incoming ocean tide. As I held our baby and remained farther up the beach, my husband and our seven, five, and four-year-old children climbed to the top of the elevated rock formation so they could get the best possible view of the Atlantic Ocean. Ali, our four-year-old, climbed up first and stood alone on the outermost edge, as he looked down at the clear, blue water. As we enjoyed ourselves in the warm sun, I was filled with a sense of tranquility. Then suddenly, everything changed.

Out of nowhere, surf waves came crashing into the rocky outcrop, hammering the children with great force. As Ali was the closest to the edge, I feared that he would be overtaken and knocked down by the waves. However, I was surprised to see that he was in a crouching position in the middle of the outcrop, as if he had been placed there after the waves hit. As my husband carefully lifted him up to bring him down to the shore, Ali began to cry. He immediately began to describe the "bright, shiny man" who picked him up and took him "to the light." He then added, "Mommy, he put me down on the rock *so* hard!" Without a shadow of doubt, I knew that my little boy's angel had stepped in to protect him. The force of the surf waves could have seriously injured him. My heart was filled with gratitude.

Connecting with Your Guardian Angel

Your guardian angel is always at your service. Since you've been gifted with the presence of this divine being, it would be wise to cultivate a relationship with your guardian. Setting aside time for linking with your angel is important. I begin each morning with meditation and prayer. In addition to requesting guidance and protection, I also ask my angel to assist me in being a beacon of love, light, and healing.

You can also begin your day by connecting with your guardian angel. Let your angel know your concerns for that day, and then request and give permission for assistance. Set an intention of being aware of and open to the guidance from your guardian angel throughout the day. Also, remember to maintain a state of appreciation for the assistance that you receive.

Guardian Angel Meditation

1. Sit in a quiet place, free from distractions.
2. Close your eyes and begin to breathe deeply. Feel the air expand in your lungs as you inhale and feel the release as you exhale.
3. Notice that any tension that you are holding in your body drifts away. You begin to feel calmer and lighter with each breath that you take.
4. When you feel centered and relaxed, place your attention at the top of your head, in the center of your skull. This is the location of the crown chakra, which is the energy center that connects you to the Universe and higher states of consciousness.
5. With your awareness stationed at the crown chakra, you may begin to feel a tingling sensation or a feeling of warmth. Connect with this energy.
6. Next, focus your awareness a few inches above your crown chakra. You should sense another area of energy and light, directly above your head.

Breathe into this energy and feel it expand. Keep your full awareness in this energy center above your head.

7. After setting the intention to connect with your guardian angel, send a silent thought to your angel, and ask them to step forward. Feel the light of your angel and bask inside the warm, glowing sphere of their love.

8. Blend with the energy of your angel and open your heart to receive any guidance that may be coming forth.

9. Be mindful that angelic communication can be subtle. Pay attention to everything that you are sensing and feeling.

10. After a few moments, thank your guardian angel for coming forward. Gently allow your awareness to come back into your physical body. Begin to move your fingers and toes slowly. As you feel more fully present in your body, slowly open your eyes.

Signs from Your Guardian Angel

Once you are regularly connecting with your guardian angel, you will receive signs that you are not alone. At your lowest point, a feather might appear out of the blue, or you might notice a repeating sequence of numbers. One of the signs that my guardian angel sends to me is the number *111*, which happens to be the exact time of my birth. Often, I notice *111* on clocks, license plates, receipts, or billboards. And whenever I do, I know that my guardian angel has received my request for guidance and that all is well. Your guardian angel may reveal a different combination of numbers specifically meaningful to you. However, the message will always be the same: "You are *never* alone. I am here with you."

Receiving visual images as messages from your angel is called *clairvoyance*. You may see pictures, symbols, or vivid colors within your mind's eye. Angels can also make their presence known by appearing objectively to the naked eye as sparkles of light, or as full-bodied apparitions. Though I tend to see angels with my inner vision much more frequently, my experience of actually seeing an angel was quite life-changing for me.

I awoke one night with the feeling that someone was in the room with me. This was strange, because my husband was at the hospital caring for a critically ill patient. Confused, I looked around our bedroom and noticed a magnificently glowing, winged figure hovering in the air. I rubbed my eyes to make sure that I was not dreaming. When I realized that I was definitely looking at an angel, I exclaimed, "Wow! Those are *huge* wings." A beautiful energy filled the room, and I wanted to remain in this glowing warmth forever. During this time of my life, I was beginning to teach angel classes. I was dealing with nagging feelings of self-doubt. When my angel appeared to me that night, my feelings of doubt dissolved. I knew that I was being divinely supported as a spiritual teacher.

Another way that your angel may communicate with you is through *clairaudience*. Angelic guidance can sound like your inner voice. Or you may hear your angel gently call your name, as if another person were speaking to you. It is important to remember that angelic guidance will always make you feel loved and supported, never judged or diminished. Sending messages through song lyrics is another way that your angel may communicate with you. My angel loves to send me messages this way!

I remember sitting and reading a book about angels in a bookstore many years ago. In the text, the author suggested that the reader should ask for a sign from their guardian angel. I followed the suggestion, not sure of what to expect. As I left the bookstore, I walked to my car and prepared to drive home. I turned on the radio, and the song *Everywhere* by Michelle Branch was playing:

"Cause you're everywhere to me

And when I close my eyes, it's you I see

You're everything I know

That makes me believe

I'm not alone.

You always light my way

I hope there never comes a day

No matter where I go

I always feel you so.

You're in everyone I see

So tell me

Do you see me?" [1]

I was blown away by the significance of the song lyrics. It was confirmation that my guardian angel heard my request.

You may also receive angelic guidance through your emotions and physical sensations. This is called *clair-sentience*. Intuitive information is often felt in the gut, or solar plexus. If you feel this area expand with joy and light, your guardian angel is letting you know that you are on the right path. On the other hand, if you get a heavy or sick feeling in the pit of your stomach, this may be your guardian angel's way of advising you to be careful or to take a different course of action.

Your guardian angel wants to see you thrive, succeed, and fully live within the vibration of love. It will become easier for you to recognize the divine guidance that is given to you when you are open to receiving signs and messages from your guardian angel. Developing a connection with your guardian angel will give you a sense of stability and security, especially during adversity. As unpredictable waves of life crash into you, your angel will hold you safely in the presence of light. So, why wait? Take the first step, develop this divine relationship, and allow the miracles to unfold.

[1] Michelle Branch, *Everywhere* (California: Maverick, 2001).

CHAPTER

Twelve

Angel Messages
By Holly Bird

HOLLY BIRD

Holly Bird is an internationally best-selling author of the book Shaken Dreams, A Journey from Wife to Caregiver, she is a mentor and life coach with a focus on aging health education and family. She shares her wealth of life experiences, everything from spiritual and family mentoring, marriage, gardening, cooking, traveling, and her favorite being a grandma on her blog.

Connect with Holly

http://www.Hollysbirdnest.com
HollyBird@hollysbirdnest.com
Facebook @hollysbirdnest
Facebook @loveyourangels Twitter @HOLLYJBIRD

Acknowledgments

To my friends and family I thank you for your continued love and support. And to my Angels both Earthly and Heavenly, I am honored and blessed for your guidance!

Angel Messages
By Holly Bird

For many years, I have felt the presence of angels. I have seen the shimmer of lights and had an overwhelming feeling of warmth when they are near. So many people want to believe but say they have never experienced anything that looks like an angel. They would know if they saw somebody with huge wings flying over or sitting on a ledge. If that were the qualification to say that you believe in angels, no one would ever believe.

Faith, for me, has always been a part of believing in angels, and doubt from others has followed me for years, but I have faith and try to explain, *"Yes, angels are in our lives whether we feel them or not. It's possible that you have experienced them and you didn't even know it."* Angels do not appear as we see them in the movies or in paintings, but angelic guidance can be so obvious that you might think it was only a coincidence, such as lights flickering, a deceased loved one coming to you in a dream, and even a direct message from a medium (a person who connects with the *"other side"*).

There are so many ways that you could be receiving a message, but angelic guidance is usually more subtle. Angels have a job, and they do it well. They are constantly drawing our attention towards signs. They will give you clues that will place you in the right direction at the right time. At first, these signs may seem small and insignificant but can increase in frequency when you are focused. Acknowledge and appreciate the messages you are receiving. My three favorite words when talking about angels: *"Ask," "Believe," and "Receive."*

If you want to feel the presence or guidance of angels, one of the easiest things you can do is to increase your awareness of them—pay attention. Knowing some of the common signs to look for will help you connect with your angels, and once you understand this, it will help you connect and communicate with your angels.

Angels frequently use people as messengers. Angels are sent to us by God to deliver messages of encouragement and inspiration, and to do this, they will use people in your life (even strangers) to tell you exactly what you need to hear in that moment. This seems to happen more when you have been struggling with a decision or issue and need some guidance to get you through it. Sometimes, a random person you meet will mention something that you desperately need to hear that you might not have otherwise heard had you not come across their path. We all have had a person who we did not know who has said something to us that made an impact. When this happens, put your phone down and start listening. That little old lady may have something to say, and your angels may be reaching out to you.

Music is another way that angels send us messages. Music is a universal language for everyone, and angels use music and lyrics to convey messages in various ways. This is often communicated through reoccurring songs. You may hear the same song playing over and over again on the radio or via your favorite way to listen to music, and wonder why. This may be an angel trying to communicate with you. Particularly, if the songs have a similar theme or come from a time in your life when the person you are thinking about (who has passed) is trying to tell you they are well. Lyrics might also help you to pick up on your intuitive feelings, or a song might lift your spirits and reassure you that everything will be okay. Not only is it important that you pay attention to this guidance through music, but it's also a perfect way to open your mind to the messages that might be in those songs.

Angels will attempt to get your attention and guide you through numbers. Some people call them "angel numbers." You may be sitting behind a car with "444" on the license plate, or you seem to look at the clock every day at "11:11" exactly. These numbers have specific meanings for you. If you are wondering about the point of seeing these numbers over and over again, think of them as signs they are sending you. It is important for us to not only look for signs from the angels, but also to be present and aware.

When you're in the presence of angels, you may get feelings of temperature changes, a coolness that may give you the chills, or a tingle or pressure in your head or the back of your neck. Sometimes, this change can come in the form of a warm, glowing feeling or light around you. This feeling could be strange the first time you are aware of it. There is no reason to be frightened because at that moment, it will feel normal and safe. The angels are there to comfort you, so there is no need to be afraid when this happens. This experience will validate that angels are with you and help you to "feel" their presence.

Angels do speak, and for those with this level of connection, it takes a high level of what is called *"vibrations"* (also known as spiritual energy) to hear the angels. Most people don't hear angel voices as an audible sound. Many people receive divine messages through nonverbal means such as visions or feelings. Some people receive messages in their mind or even hear a voice whispering to them, and it seems to appear out of thin air. If this has happened to you, you may be receiving guidance from your angels. Hearing the guidance of your angels is a wonderful sign of their presence, and often occurs when you need comfort, reassurance, or angelic guidance. If you hear a faint voice and wonder what it said, ask the angels to repeat their message. Listen with your heart and your mind. They want you to be able to understand. They will repeat what they said—just listen.

Have you ever noticed a particular smell, a fuzzy-looking shape or sound, and have not been able to identify the source? This could show up in the form of a lovely, sweet scent or a ringing in your ear. Because we often question what is called our sixth sense, these types of messages come through various sights, sounds, and smells, and can be obvious. If you are aware and paying attention, seeing angel shapes in the clouds, sparks of lights and electrical interruptions are also signs that angels are near. This often occurs as a confirmation that you should be listening to your intuition. Sometimes the scent of different flowers can be smelled when there are none around, and this can be a sign that angels are present to help calm you in a time of need.

Once you begin to tune into the signs from your angels and practice the present moment of awareness, you will become more conscious of your angels and the guidance and assistance they are offering to you. If you notice any of these signs, be aware of the message they may be trying to send you. The first step is to let the angels know that you want and need their assistance. They will not interfere if they are not wanted.

Take time to learn about your angels. You can ask them their names by quietly meditating and asking, *"What is your name?"* Usually, the first name you hear is your angel's name who you are communicating with. Try not to doubt because you have never known anyone with that name. We were all assigned an angel as our guardian the day we were born, and this angel is not someone you would have known. But other angels can and do appear, and when your vibrations are high enough, you will directly receive messages from Archangel Michael, Gabriel, and Uriel. You never know who has a message for you!

I know that not everyone believes that anyone can communicate with angels, but you can. You are loved, and the guidance of your angels is right there with you every day!

The best time to begin connecting with your angels is anytime! It seems that the first time people think about asking for guidance is when their lives are in turmoil, and I say, "Definitely ask!" The best time to learn and spiritually connect is when you are calm and emotionally open to "connect." Connecting with your angels is like any other relationship. The more you listen and spend time focusing on the relationship, the stronger the connection will become, and you will receive and understand the messages with ease and clarity.

Angels are spiritual beings of unconditional love and light, so when you consciously tune in with love and openness, it will make connecting easier and help the energy flow from the angels to you and through you. Starting with a mind-clearing and calming meditation can help you to open your mind and your heart to receive the guidance and messages that the angels are communicating with you.

The basic idea of meditation is to focus on your breathing. Do not think about anything but your breath. Every time your mind begins to shift away from your breath and you get lost in thought, bring your attention back to your breath. Repeat this until your meditation timer sounds. Every time you bring your attention back to your breath, you work out your "attention muscle." Over time, your focus, concentration, and attention span will improve, and you will be able to enjoy the benefits that so many people receive from meditation.

I struggled in the beginning with meditation, but I knew it was good for me. My mind was doing its own thing, not focusing on the way I was meditating. This is normal. Take some time to clear your mind so that you train your brain to stay focused. It can help your mind *defragment* your thoughts so you can make better sense of them and be able to step away from them to gain perspective. You will also be more aware of your everyday surroundings and be more open to communicating with your angels.

The most important way for you to communicate with your angels is to be open. Your angels are already with you. Their unconditional presence can be summoned at any time, depending on your willingness to let them and their higher vibration into your life. An angel's main role is to help you get through spiritual difficulties, and also to help you celebrate joy!

Invoking: *Calling on angels.* Think or call out and say, *"I need you."* Your angels are there for you. When my husband was ill and I needed help desperately, as he lay in his hospital bed in our den. I had been awake for days, asking (almost begging) the angels to be there for me.

I went to go lie down in the living room so that I would be close to the den, but I could still lie in the dark and get some rest. I had been lying down for about twenty minutes and had started to doze off when I got a chill. As I opened my eyes, the room was glowing with a golden light. I focused my eyes and realized that I was seeing angels appear before me. It was not like big wings flying around; it was an essence and a knowing, and the beauty and peacefulness that came over me will be with me forever. I quietly got up and went in to check on my husband. The nurse was sitting in the corner, reading a book. She asked me sharply why I wasn't resting. I told her that I felt angels, and they were coming to take my husband. She set her book down and said, "I am a very spiritual person, but your husband probably has weeks before he is going anywhere." I knew better. I had been around when others had passed and had felt this feeling. I had never seen the angels glow like I did this time. I knew she was wrong. I sat down in my husband's recliner and started to cry. The nurse came over and comforted me, telling me I was just overtired and that she only had a little bit of time before she had to leave. She said, "Just lie here in the recliner and close your eyes." As I closed my eyes, I could feel the angels, the presence was a comfort and I drifted off to sleep. It seemed as if only a few minutes had passed when she woke me. She said that that my husband's oxygen was low, so she'd turned it up, and not to give him any more medicine until five. She had given him everything, and I could probably go back to sleep; he should be fine.

I thanked her, and she left. My husband was making a very strange noise. It wasn't the "death rattle" I had heard from others who passed away. It was as if he was mumbling, and I figured he was talking in his sleep. Maybe the nurse was right, but my gut feeling was not so sure. Exhausted, I fell back asleep, but fifteen minutes later, I was awakened by a crashing noise—I jumped up. I couldn't find anything, but I noticed that my husband was a little blue. I turned up his oxygen and sat and watched him breathe. He was barely breathing. I sat on the bed and held his hand. Sitting there, I could feel the angels and knew it was getting close. A smile came across his face, a true smile that I hadn't seen since he was diagnosed with Parkinson's. I could tell he was leaving me and I knew the angels had been there guiding me and my husband.

No matter the situation, your angels are there for you, helping to guide you through good times and bad. Even in my fear of not wanting to lose the love of my life, there were so many messages, a glowing room, crashing noises to wake me up, and a feeling of warmth at the time of death of 4:44 a.m.

CHAPTER

Thirteen

Not All Angels Have Wings
By JamieLynn

JAMIELYNN

JamieLynn is a two-time best-selling author, a public speaker, mother of two, and CEO of Arise Empowered, LLC. Of Having endured sexual assault as a child by five family members, JamieLynn spent ten years working on personal development and leadership training, transforming her life from survivor to thriver. Out of her transformation, she founded Arise Empowered, LLC., whose mission of empowering lives one voice at a time, offers products, courses and empowerment coaching around sexual assault. A trained public speaker, JamieLynn delivered a talk on thriving after sexual abuse at DEBx in Tempe, Arizona. She hosts Awareness Talks, the Empowerment Program, and the

Breakthrough & Thrive Summit. Through her healing and discovering her voice, JamieLynn saw that she was making a difference for others and has chosen to lead others in finding their path to healing. A seeker and mystic, JamieLynn also provides energy healings.

Acknowledgments

To devote time to healing and training it takes a community to live a created life. I have had many coaches, friends and family in support of my path. To you the readers, may your path be filled with love. To my parents and in-laws, thank you for your love. To all my LM coaches and friends, my integrity and authenticity is amazing, and you caused it! To Melissa Z, Rob, Gordon, Davy, Christal H., Melissa M. To my sister Laurie, and brother Steven. To my large family, for all the talks and experiences. You are all amazing and I love you deeply. To my editor Vicky! To my husband Mike, my partner and best friend. Thank you for loving me for who I am unconditionally. Of course, to my little princesses who will change the world too, Jalynn and Freya. Lots of love to you all.

Not All Angels Have Wings
By JamieLynn

It was the first night in my new room, the first room of the house, which to me felt like a magical place. My childhood was going well so far. I was starting to notice things about life, and not wanting to let go of childhood fancies, yet, learning of reality.

It's 1992. I had recently turned seven, and was playing with my favorite toys as the moon's light brightly rained through the three windows of my new room. A few toys: Barbie, her RV, and all the needed camping essentials. My eyes began to get heavy when I heard my name being called from down the long empty hallway. I could not define who it was, so after the third time of hearing my name, I decided to check it out. I made my way down the long dark hall, and followed the winding stairs to the kitchen where my mother and my aunt where talking about work. My aunt, my mom's best friend, lived with us in the last room of the hallway. It was nice because without her, I would have been afraid to be upstairs all alone.

"Hi Mom, did you call for me?" I asked with a long yawn. "Honey, we thought you were asleep." Mom wrapped her arm around me and squeezed. "Okay, just checking. Sleep sounds good. Goodnight Mom, goodnight Auntie Terrie." I kissed each of them on the cheek and made my way to my room.

Once I got back to my room, I heard my name being called once more. Now fully awake and heart racing, I turned off my light, ran to my bed and pulled the covers over my face to hide. Not fully moved into my room yet, the only night light was the moon, which left deep shadows in each of the corners.

I felt as if my room was full of people—twelve, I think. I peeked over the covers to find my room empty, then a light haze of figures came into view. Tall and non-defined, they stood hovering a few inches off the floor. I could make out faces and maybe long, silky gowns. They bobbed as though they were a cluster of floating buoys in the waters of Lake Michigan, and were lit up enough to know they were there, but not so much to be blinding.

A boy stood behind them leaning on the edge of my closet at the far end of the room, I knew him, or it felt like I did. Before my sister was born, when I was three, I called him "Boyfriend." My mother told me he was imaginary. Could this be real? Could it truly be him? Where had he been all this time, and why did he go away?

"You realized I wasn't genuinely there, and after that, you didn't need me anymore, well, until today," the boy said without moving his lips. "Oh, and yeah, this is all real, you asked for it, so here we are. Listen to them, you are safe, we all love you more than you know." Okay, I thought, I will listen. "Good, because they can't stay long," he answered my thoughts. The boy was my age, and I remembered he had always looked my age. Strange, I thought.

"You asked us to come, to remind you, so that this time you would not forget." This voice was different; it didn't sound like a child, it was older and slower, and not male or female. "What was I before I was here, was there something?

Or was there nothing?" I whispered, quickly realizing that even a whisper was too loud and continued to talk with my mind instead. Of course, later, I learned this is called telepathy.

One spoke for them all, "We are here to remind you of what you must do in this life. You were given many chances. Each time you failed to follow through with your promise to us and to this world. This is the last chance you have to complete your task, or you will never come back to this plane again."

Images flashed in my mind of other lifetimes, lots of them. In one life I wore tight clothes that didn't fit well, my body was skinny and in shape, but my mind was messed up, and there were many men taking something of me and tossing money at my sad lump of a body.

In other lives, I was a farmer's wife or a teacher with children. Life was great, and yet it felt empty, something was missing, I couldn't be happy. In another life, I was famous, but for all the wrong reasons. I was having fun, and I didn't care what I was supposed to be doing here. All of them, the good and the bad, they were all wrong. I was missing the point—I had failed to keep the promise that I had volunteered to perform.

Then lastly, I saw myself in a bright area, wearing a shimmering gown. I was older, with long blond hair that sparkled. I was extremely serious and confident, and I was speaking to an older man who was dressed the same, with a peach mist and clouds settled at our feet.

"What would make a difference this time?" The man asks.

"Remind me when I am young, make me remember, offer me gifts of the life to look forward to and have them come true. Listen to my cries. Let me know you are there, and when I am ready, have the energy flow so that it is easy to find my way. All of these are reminders of what I am saying here, and to remember the past lives where I failed. To remember the importance of what it is I must do for the sake of others." It felt like this was in a distant past and nowhere here on earth.

Back in my room as a seven-year-old girl, they stand to ask me what I need to succeed.

"We are prepared to gift you paths that will assist you in being successful in this life, all you need to do is ask. We are always listening. It is strange how when we take on human form, we forget so easily that we have this access. For you, however, you will remember, and there will be times where you forget." They laid out the rules of what to expect. "How can we assist you? We can tell you it all. Your next ten years of life is mapped out, and we can tell you," they offered.

"No! Please, I mean, please don't tell me all of it. I fear I know the energy all too well, and not knowing is better. I think in one life you told me it all, and that is why my life was so sad."

I took a moment to think, what if I had something to look forward to? Something that I knew was going to happen and it would be so wonderful it was worth waiting for?

"Can I have a daughter, a beautiful and creative little girl who is half me and half her father—to be fair. She will think like me and play like I do. She will understand me and the work I need to do, in some way she will understand. I will love her and protect her and treat her better than how I have been treated. My mom seems to hate me, I don't want her to know that pain. I want her to be smarter and better than me. Oh, and she will never have glasses!" I asked, nearly crying.

I felt her soul was already waiting for me, and I wished so much that I could have her now. She could be my best friend. But then she would not be mine. I wanted to be the one to raise her and guide her, so I would have to wait.

"It is done. Could you do us, the universe, a favor? We have a soul here who wants to be your daughter too." They asked.

"No way, my mother goes nuts with two. How do you think I would be any better? She always tells us in her next life she will not have any kids, and she raised her brothers, so why does she have to raise us. I don't want to be so angry. So, no, only one."

A little face comes into my view. She kind of looks how my sister did, chubby cheeks and bright blond curly hair. Her eyes as blue as the sky. "Can you be my mommy? I promise I will be really good for you mommy, promise." It was the voice of a toddler. Her voice was pure and sweet. Through her eyes, mostly, I felt her soul. I wanted so much to squish them both between my arms, and I felt I would be a wonderful mother.

"Ok, fine, but give me five years in between—for my sanity." I pouted with tears in my eyes.

"It is done, is there anything else? Normally we are asked about money," they laughed with surprise.

"Oh, money would be good, but you know, I want to earn it. If I am going to get a million dollars, I don't want to blow it. I want to respect it, so let me earn it," I requested.

"It is done, is there anything else?"

"Yes, one more thing, I am sure I will have others as I go along—things I can't think of now—but this one is important. To have someone that goes through all of this with me. Who doesn't get mad at me for what I need to do, and maybe they even come out on the other side supporting the work. Can I have that?" I felt the excitement build up.

"Yes, we have someone in mind, we need to do some checking first. We are always listening, so ask us whatever you need. However, there will be a time when it seems we are not here, it will seem that the universe has turned its back to you. It will seem you are alone. In that portion of time, you may begin to forget us, you may forget your promise. As you have already requested, we will send little reminders when the time is right. It does not mean we have turned our backs to you, it does not mean we cannot hear you nor does it mean we are not there. That will be a time of pain and a time to be by yourself."

As I drifted off to sleep still "talking" to them, they left one at a time, and I heard them say, "You will make a difference for millions upon millions." I had no concept of what a million people was and still I knew it was going to be amazing, generations to come would benefit from this work. The work was important. I already understood that I am the vessel; it wasn't about me.

Over the years, I knew to hide what was told to me. If I were to go around telling everyone I was going to have these two girls and it turned out to be true, my child mind feared the government or someone testing my brain and I would have no time left for my promise. I was assured that I had the potential to even levitate, but that again was not my promise for this life. I also didn't want people picking on me for my predictions. I kept it all to myself and allowed my human emotions to dictate what I was going to say.

In time I learned to call them *guiding spirits*. I learned of angels, but I knew guiding spirits were different. They had lived lives, many lives. They knew things of being in physical form that an angel could not know due to lack of experience. I wasn't sure if angels were made up or if they were real. I had never seen one, and I wasn't sure if I had ever experienced one. I learned as an adult that angels are at our sides as much as our guides are, and all we need to do is speak to them. Let them know we can feel their love, and we are grateful for their guidance.

Some of us have been chosen due to a promise we made before birth. We choose our parents, our location, and our ethnicity. We are here for the experience; we collect these experiences and bring them back to the other side. That, I believe, is why we are so vastly different. Why a baby can be struck with cancer and a felon can be full of life and healthy. We are here to experience it all. One thing I learned is that when we don't forgive ourselves, we carry that with us from one life to another, and even in this life, we carry that from one moment to the next.

Our angels, guiding spirits, and spirit animals don't want us to live in fear, anger, resentment, and hate. They wish and pray for us to feel whole and live our lives fully. They are here to guide us. This is why you hear stories of people committing horrible crimes, and then they come back and teach healing ways. Or why someone with cancer is healed. Forgiveness and love are there. Understanding and acceptance. We all need these things, and first, we start with ourselves. We ask for guidance and love for our wounds, and then as we heal, we can show others the path to healing as well.

I will save the story of the hard times for another book. In the end, I have become the Founder and CEO of Arise Empowered LLC, a company that gives a voice through empowering others to speak up, share their stories of abuse and trauma, and heal. I host the Breakthrough & Thrive Summit, which allows the viewer to ignite their power, take charge of their healing, and create their happiness after having experienced sexual abuse and trauma. By encourage-ing holistic healing, there is an openness to the energy of our bodies and for those around us, including our angels and spirit guides. They can help us heal and guide us to the right paths we need at the time, if only we listen to them.

Close your eyes and ask a simple question. If the answer feels pure and good, they are talking to you. Thank them for all they have done, for the care and love they bring you, and allow yourself to feel that love as they answer you.

Lots of love to you all. Listen, and you will be guided.

CHAPTER

Fourteen

Connecting With
Your Angels
By Kim Purcell

KIM PURCELL

Kim Purcell is a wellness workshop facilitator and self care coach. Married for 18 years to Ken Purcell, they have three thriving teenage children. Kim worked in publishing for 15 years, where she developed her passion for nutrition. Diagnosed with Crohn's/Colitis over 20 years ago, Kim healed herself through nutrition. Having overcome assault as a teenager—an eating disorder was one of many self-sabotaging behave-iors—Kim thrived through in her progression toward wellness. Kim worked in the nutrition field, until the gift of her latest wellness work landed in her lap. Kim has been working with women and teen girls on their journeys toward mind, body, and spiritual wellness in Ponte Vedra Beach, Florida. She jokes that she is more likely certifiable than certified, and she would love to invite you into her huge loving heart to help in any way she can. Find her on www.facebook.com/thrivetribekp or email: agehealthier@gmail.com.

Acknowledgments

Special thanks to all my sisters who have let me into your hearts to guide in whatever way I could toward your self-healing. It has been an honor and a dream to work with you and your daughters. I cherish your faith and trust in me. Thank you to Lee McCormick and Jorge Luis Delgado for sharing your wisdom and your teachings with me, and to all my teachers and mentors over the years who have helped me grow. Thank you mostly to my friends and family, especially to my mother, Joanne Droge and my father, Dr. Edward F. Droge, Jr., Ed.D. Dad, a special thank you for your countless hours of editing. To my beautiful husband, Ken Purcell, my in-laws, and my children, Bryce, Darby, and Parker, thank you for loving me through it all.

Connecting With Your Angels
By Kim Purcell

To this day, I can still see the luminous blue of her silky gown and feel the warmth of her loving presence. A profound peace and sense of protection filled the room. For a lifetime, I have cherished that peaceful, loving feeling, that way a mother loves her young child, with full acceptance, protection, understanding, and encouragement. Over time, my mind made sense of what happened. I came to believe it was my mother, so beautiful in her billowing blue nightgown wafting through my room that night, probably to tuck me in. Only recently did I discover it was not actually my mom. She insists she never had a blue nightgown. Still, to this day, that color is unmistakably the most beautiful royal blue I've ever seen; the silky way it shimmered in the light. That color was real. The experience was real. But, if it wasn't my mother, who was it? I believe now that it was Mother Mary. Born and raised Catholic, the Virgin Mother was ever-present for me. My mother looked similar then to the pictures we see of Mary, a flawless beauty about her that was truly divine. It makes sense that I thought it was her. It was undeniably maternal love I felt. Mom and I dissected the memory, the time and place, and every nightgown she ever owned. We know it wasn't her.

Looking back, that was my first vision of an angel. Fast forward 25 years—I had the angel visit that changed my life. Days after my best friend died from her battle with cancer, I decided to do a cancer walk on the beach as my goodbye. I had two young babies, one in his stroller, and my daughter, six weeks old, snug in my body pouch as I walked. It was a perfect Florida February day. The air was cool and still. But I was still so raw. So, sometime about halfway, I turned to head back alone. I needed time to be with my pain, alone; to talk to my friend in Heaven. I had this heavy longing to be with her, once more. I talked to her, silently saying everything I prayed I had said well enough while she was alive. Then, right there in the midst of my grieving, the heavy hole in my chest was filled with the most divine sense of soothing warmth and serenity. It comforted me in a way that defies explanation. For a moment, I got lost in a dance with that divine feeling of love, knowing my angel, my precious Lisa, was sending this heartwarming, healing hush from Heaven. To this day, I can connect with my Lisa's love and still feel a hint of that heavenly hug, that beloved moment in time, when she reached down to me and merged her divine grace with me in my grief. Oh, how my soul is warmed, sharing this story with you.

That heavenly hug on the beach shifted my under-standing of what is always available to us, even, if not especially in our darkest moments. It taught me we could connect with loved ones who've passed. It brought peace and love beyond understanding to my grief, and unclogged the congestion in my connection to my angels. As if some powerful potentiality imprisoned in me was finally freed and flowing. Mind you, I take a linguist's liberty with the semantic meaning of the word angel, coming from the Greek word *angelos*, meaning messengers. If angels are mess-engers from Heaven, for me, that includes our dearly departed.

My connection to my angels came serendipitously until I made it a practice. Most of what I know about when angels speak has been a direct divine download. To this day, I have never felt alone again. There, in the nexus between our deepest grief and our most profound love, lies an invitation from grace to connect. Love is everlasting. Surrounded by angels in this multiverse, our multi-dimensional universe, we are never alone. When we are connected to our ancestors, we live a better life. Envision the ever-presence of our ancestors, witnessing, guarding, guiding. As Richard Rohr says, "It is Heaven all the way to Heaven." We choose to live a better life, or forever live the life we chose. In the company of angels, our thoughts, patterns, and actions become pure and right.

How to Connect

Fundamentalists advise that connection with angels should never be initiated by us; they will make themselves known when they need to be heard. Catholics teach that the departed are accessible, among the Communion of Saints. I respectfully incorporate the Almighty into the connection to keep communication free and clear of any unholy entities. Where there is good, there is bad. We 'don't go in sloppy.' We mind our attention as we connect, bathed in and protected by the light of the Holy Spirit, your inner Buddha or your higher self. Whatever you call it, bring your God into your connection always. We don't want to connect with any of His fallen angels.

God gives us the gift of discernment. We can distinguish someone's specific energetic whisper of love. When we learn to trust our intuitive gifts, like the gift of discernment, we can know who is connecting with us. We can continue to experience the blessings of our departed's love. Love is everlasting.

Learning to Listen

Find a quiet place, where you can silence the busyness of your mind. Maybe it's near the water. Maybe your only quiet place is a tiny space you've uncluttered in your closet, where you can be uninterrupted and silence the world around you. Maybe it's lying in bed, eyes closed in that space between wake and sleep. Find your place to quiet your mind.

With eyes closed, notice the light in the area of your third eye. Imagine that light extending outside yourself into the space that is your aura. It is there the holies in Heaven live, not some far off space on a cloud or in a temple somewhere. There, just outside your physical body, is the etheric realm, where angels live. Allow the light to expand and merge with that field around you.

Be open to signs and learn what they mean. Many signs are universal. A heart, we know, means love. But there is deeper work to discover how that divine message of love applies in that moment. Is it to love yourself, or to share love in a relationship? Maybe the angels are telling you that you are loved. Learn to trust your knowing. With practice comes clarity. Another common sign is wings. Wings remind you angels are present. It may come to mean that it's time for you to 'take flight,' or get something you've wanted to do off the ground. Classic emoji signs are another universal message. A smiley face may be your angels' way of sharing divine joy or encouragement. A sad face can be a sign of consolation. Angels come to soothe our sorrow and remind us it is okay to be sad. We are not alone in our sadness. Initially, the signs will be for you, but in time with regular spiritual connection work, the sad face might indicate someone close to you is experiencing sadness. Always check in with yourself first. Our angels are here to help us lift our souls and live our true life purpose. It's important to take time after a sign, however it comes to you—a vision, a shape, a message you heard or felt, or a sudden epiphany. Take quiet time to be with the message and allow its meaning to unfold.

Repeated numbers are another common sign. Whether it's 222, 3:33 or $11.11, any time you see repeated numbers, check in with your angels. It is not a coincidence. Allow the gentle whisper to remind you to tap into the ever-present guidance of your angels. Often this happens in the middle of the night. Use that time to clear your mind of its usual chatter and do your lightwork of connecting with your angels. Often you will fall back asleep gently with a message in the morning.

What you think or feel the signs mean is important. The message itself is what it is. What happens thereafter is the story we attach to it, written in our mind. But, if you stay in tune with the God-light connection, you will be guided to allow its meaning to come through with divine wisdom and discernment.

Use gratitude as a vibrational path to your higher self. If you are not used to speaking in terms of frequency or vibration, think quantum physics. We are all energy. Our thoughts are energy. Our emotions are energy. Gratitude and love are among the highest vibrations on this plane and bring us closest to the angelic realm. Use gratitude and love as tools to start learning to listen to your inner voice. Gratitude brings acceptance and peace into your life. That too, is intimately entwined with staying connected to your angels.

Remember you are not crazy! Years ago, I scratched the surface of my connection to my angels a little deeper, doing ancient Native American spiritual work with several shamans. It was as if I had unhinged the lid off a volcano and the signs were flowing everywhere. On fire with the light of God, the messages overflowed out of me and to me like lava swallowing a mountain. For years, I worked with my mentors to decipher the messages; to master my connection. Eventually, it did calm down. But I assure you, I thought I was crazy! I heard messages loud and clear from trees, insects, sea creatures, encounters with birds, everywhere I turned. Sure I doubted myself. Did I just smell my grandfather's cologne? We all doubt the messages at first. That is natural. We have all looked over our shoulder; asked ourselves if we were making this up. Self-doubt is part of the human experience and will creep into your practice. A speck of sparkling glitter floated by, then disappeared. Your camera caught glowing orbs of light. You felt a sudden change in temperature and a presence; guided in a direction. The electronics in your house went haywire. You heard a voice or somehow knew. Most of us have been trained not to listen to those quiet knowing voices, that whisper in our soul, that even shouts to be heard. We are more trained *not* to see than *how* to see. The knowing that follows is like the "A-ha!" of a child, the epiphany of clear, direct communication. Practice trusting that knowing feeling. Self-doubt will simmer down. We are all capable of infinitely more than we have ever been told. The long and short of it is, we have had the wisdom we seek all along. If you find yourself feeling crazy, find a spiritual mentor whose heart is pure to help you. You will know them when you find them.

Have you ever heard a song at the right moment that gave you the answer you were looking for? That is not a coincidence—it's the velvet glove of your angel guiding your attention to listen right at that moment, to hear the answer. I will never forget living in New Jersey, wondering for months if I should move to Florida to live with my boyfriend, now my husband. One morning, I heard the song on the radio *With Arms Wide Open* by Creed. I felt it deep in my soul; the words were crystal clear. "It seems my life is going to change. I close my eyes, begin to pray. Then tears of joy stream down my face." The message was clear. My life was going to change. Tears of joy streamed down my face all the way to work that day. My decision was made. There was no questioning that message from my angels.

Nature is an abundant source of angel whispers. Quiet yourself in nature and witness. Messages in clouds, chance encounters with animals or insects. Even a blade of grass that seems to stand alone, dancing and waving, in a still green meadow as if to say, "Hello! I see you! Can you see me?" Waving like the big blowup stick figure outside a business, that single blade of grass is a sign. We can all find shapes in nature, but messages from angels are different. They grab your gaze, as if your attention was directed by something outside yourself—like a giant, velvety glove on the hand of an angel shifted your focus, swiftly, and purposefully.

When angels speak, their messages are pure and often simple. Heavenly, their messages are inherently from goodness. They may be stern, directive, even admonishing; they guide and guard. They never direct toward harm. If you are having those thoughts, seek help to quiet them. They are surely not from your guardian angels. Angel messages can include:

1. I am safe.

2. I am okay.

3. I am love.

4. Love is eternal.

5. We are not alone.

6. Amplifying gratitude.

7. Feeding inspiration.

8. Feeding belief in ourselves, our path, or give guidance with a specific situation.

9. Illuminating life purpose.

We are led through the darkness to the light within ourselves. The wisdom we seek, we already have. The connection between our inner spirit and our outer angels is like a complete circle—perfect and never-ending. Like anything new, inseparable connection builds with practice over time. Eventually, the light will guide you with or without your specific intention. Staying open to the messages is the beginning of a practice of learning to hear the messages of the angels. Pay attention to the signs. Listen for the whispers. As God is ever-present, so are the messengers. Called or not called, they are here for us. Most of them we miss with our autopilot blinders on. The work is to wake up and witness. When we play in nature, take time to be present and harmonize with the pace of nature, abandoning the rush of our world, if only briefly each day, it becomes easier to hear the messages from your angels. Surely, they will continue until they are heard. They break through our vibrational veil and do more than the gentle tap with the velvet glove. When we miss message after message, they figuratively bonk us over the head. Our angels will shout their message out loud, calling our name, somehow getting our attention, maybe in a vivid dream, or through songs, numbers, animals, or nature. They put feathers in unexpected places, give rainbows without the rain, lucid dreams, vivid smells. Learn to trust those still, small voices. "Lead us not into temptation." They inspire us with good thoughts to heal, to protect, to console, to comfort.

Until we wake up to the opportunity to connect with our angels for guidance and wisdom, hope and healing, consolation and love, their messages might remain hidden. Once we begin to see that the messages are everywhere, they are radically revealed in everything.

CHAPTER

Fifteen

Angels Of The Five Elements
By Kira Murphy

KIRA MURPHY

Kira Murphy is a nationally and state board-certified acupuncturist, with a Master of Science in Oriental Medicine; the master graduate program lasted four and a half years. She owns a storefront named Ki Healing Center, in Denver, Colorado (Ki-Denver.com), offering various types of healing treatments, both on-site and distance. Kira is an author in the best-selling book, *Healer*. She practices gentle acupuncture and esoteric healing, incorporating various styles from which she has studied. Some examples are Jin Shin Jyutsu, Reiki Master Teacher, Medical Qi Gong, Celtic shamanism, five elements, crystal healing, and quantum energy medicine. Kira can obtain and draw a person's unique, one of a kind, sacred power symbol through meditation. Although Kira has been a healer since childhood, she has been formally practicing since about 2007. To find out your sacred soul symbol, follow MySacredSymbol on social media.

Acknowledgments

Thank you to my angels: my parents, brother, and daughter for always being my earth angels.

Angels Of The Five Elements
By Kira Murphy

Angels are imagined, seen, interacted with, and honored in numerous ways for people. Some people believe in the ethereal, human-like form with the white cloth, halo, and beautiful, feathered wings. Some people believe in guardian angels. Some people believe in archangels, such as Archangels Michael, Gabriel, and Ezekiel. Some people believe our ancestors or passed on loved ones' energy is still around us, giving us support or signs when needed, and they are the angels in our lives. Some people believe there are earthbound angels living in our reality disguised as humans, helping us every day. Some people use the word to describe a person who is helpful, loving, or special to them. Or they use it to describe surgeons and people who save lives. There are various ways to think about angels and interact with them in our lives.

I, personally, believe in aspects of all of these. It is up to our individual perspective to decide what is meaningful and what speaks to us. Just like some people are great at different skills and ways of learning, everyone individually attuned to interpreting the help from angels in ways that resonate with us. One thing is certain, there is energy and loving light out there, and within yourself, that wants to be of assistance, that wants to help, to be called upon, to be heard/seen/felt/interpreted in some way.

How we choose to connect with angels is limitless. Some people have abilities to see, hear, feel, or even talk with angels. We may not all have these abilities, but one thing we do all have is the connection to Mother Earth and the five elements. The five elements and the five element angels I will be speaking of are fire, water, earth, metal, and wood.

Nature and the elements of our home planet, Earth, is something we all live in and can connect or reconnect with easily. With technology so accessible and increasing at such a rapid rate, sometimes we forget to tap into our true nature and spend time with the elements that support, create, and sustain life. We all experience the five elements in some way each day. Even our body is comprised of meridians corresponding to the five elements, which influence specific organ systems and emotions. We have an inherent connection with Mother Earth. We are Mother Earth's children. Earth can live without us, but we cannot live without it. No other planet that we know of can sustain our human lives. That is one of the reasons why I feel that we can all connect with the elements in both a physical and spiritual way to interact with angels.

When I speak of angels, it is up to you to translate the information into a form that is meaningful to you. Angels to me mean helpers, energetic support, love light, or a positive presence we can interact with and call upon. I have worked with the five elements in energy work for over 15 years, and I believe relating the elements with angel messages is something everyone can do if they know what to look for and pay attention.

"Ever felt an angel's breath in the gentle breeze? A teardrop in the falling rain? Hear a whisper against the rustle of leaves? Or been kissed by a lone snowflake? Nature is an angel's favorite hiding place." Carrie Latet

There are angels, spirits, energies, or helpers of these elements constantly orchestrating for the highest good and evolution of our physical health and spiritual evolution.

Below, I am going to name some characteristics and traits of the element and the corresponding angel. The main correspondences and associations include, but are certainly not limited to, season, direction, development stage, numbers, grains, animals, domestic animals, planet, yin organ, yang organ, color, sound, smell, emotion, taste, tissue, sense organ, and climate. It's my wish that by naming these associations, you will start to notice the signs and synchronicities of the five element angels that are within us and around us at all times. When you see a negative emotion listed, know that this is not the emotion of the angel. It is the emotion the angel can help you transform. It's a guide to choosing the angel who would be best suited to give your attention to or call upon.

I will also give random examples of actions you can take to connect with your element and element angel. By understanding the characteristics of the element, you can then recognize which angel is around you and showing up for you. Or which angel would be most helpful to assist you in specific areas of life.

In addition, I will be providing examples of signs and signals from angels of that element. These are only examples. Signs can come in more forms than can be listed or imagined, and are different for each individual. Use these to spark ideas and understand but be open to anything! Angels work in mysterious and sometimes unexpected ways. The more open you are, the more you can fast track your assistance and connection and evolve on this path of joy and love.

When you are connecting, have your prayer, gratitude, thanks, question, goals, and wishes in mind, and then look for signs and give thanks when you receive them. It can take practice to perceive them and time to rewire the brain to be aware of these love light signs. Get creative; don't doubt yourself. Angels are waiting to help and connect. Even if you don't think you received a sign, know they are there supporting you and working for your highest good. You can also close your eyes and use your imagination. Our imagination is an extremely powerful tool that is the ignition to create in our physical world.

Five Element Angel of Fire

Characteristics: Summer, south, growth, numbers two and seven, beans, birds, foul, Mars, heart, small intestine, red, laughing, scorched, joy, love, honor, cruelty, impatience, arrogance, bitter, blood vessels, tongue, heat, and 11:00 a.m.-3:00 p.m.

Action ideas: Do something that brings you joy. Ride a roller coaster. Watch a comedy and laugh. Face the direction south and ask angels your question. Put on red lipstick or wear a red scarf. Go to a bird sanctuary or bird watch. Light a candle and meditate while gazing into the flame.

Signs of Angel of Fire interaction: Things keep showing up in pairs. A bird flies or you hear a bird as you are connecting with angels. You get a whiff of something scorched or a sudden bitter taste in your mouth. Someone sticks their tongue out at you playfully.

"Fire is the energy of summer; it gives us warmth and the capacity to love and be loved. It enables us to mature and blossom." Neil Gumenick

Five Element Angel of Water

Characteristics: Winter, north, storage, numbers one and six, millet, shell-covered animals like a tortoise or a crab, pig, Mercury, kidney, bladder, black, grunting, putrid, gentleness, fear, salty, bones, ears, cold, and 3:00 p.m.-7:00 p.m.

Action ideas: Play in the snow or make snow angels. Enjoy millet bread. Make a pattern with seashells. Go to an animal farm and feed the pigs. Wear all black clothes. Make art or a magic wand with found bones. Take an Epsom salt bath. Go for a swim, put your feet in the water, or get in a float tank or cryotherapy.

Signs of Angel of Water interaction: It begins to snow or rain. You see a turtle logo or art. You hear or see the name, Mercury. You hear a grunt. You feel fearful, then get a sense of courage or comfort. Your ears tingle, or like that old saying, "I can feel it in my bones."

"Water brings the elements full circle. It gives us adaptability and will-power. It is the element of winter, giving us time to pause and gather strength. It is the seedbed of all life." Neil Gumenick

Five Element Angel of Earth

Characteristics: Any season or no season, center, trans-formation, numbers five and ten, rice, human, ox, Saturn, spleen, stomach, yellow, singing, fragrant, compassion, fairness, worry or pensiveness, sweet, muscles, mouth and lips, dampness, and 7:00 a.m.-11:00 a.m.

Action ideas: Transform something old into something new. Repurpose an item. Decorate something ugly and make it beautiful. Say a mantra, prayer, or wish five or ten times. Enjoy a sweet treat. Exercise and strengthen or stretch your muscles. Exfoliate and moisturize your mouth/lips, or apply a sweet lip balm, draw a circle in the sand or dirt and stand in the center. Walk barefoot on Mother Earth.

Signs of Angel of Earth interaction: You encounter a song, movie, or book with Saturn in it. You see something with a ring around it. You see the color yellow in unusual places. Your sense of worry is lifted. Someone offers you a sweet dessert or candy. You hear someone singing or get invited to a concert. You hear a song with a message that answers your question or gives you a message. You get a gut feeling or butterflies in your stomach. You see brand names or labels with the name Ox in it.

"Earth is the energy of late summer; it gives us the ability to nurture ourselves and others. It provides our center and represents our mother." Neil Gumenick

Five Element Angel of Metal

Characteristics: Autumn, west, harvest, numbers four and nine, hemp, mammals, dog, Venus, lung, large intestine, white, weeping, rotten, courage, righteousness, sadness, grief, pungent, skin, nose, dryness, and 3:00 a.m.-7:00 a.m.

Action ideas: With gratitude in your heart, harvest fruits and veggies from a garden. Play with or walk a dog. Volunteer at a dog rescue. Do deep breathing exercises. Place attention on breath and lung expansion. Use your nose to enjoy your favorite flower or fragrances. Give your skin a treatment/renewal with essential oils, exfoliation, moisturizer, or dry brush your skin. Let the sun shine on your skin and feel the warmth. Wear your favorite metal jewelry.

Signs of Angel of Metal interaction: You see leaves falling or changing colors. You see the number nine or four repeating on license plates, clocks, receipts, or anywhere else. When you're feeling sad, something or someone comes in to cheer you up or give you a hug. You stumble upon an amazing skincare product. You suddenly smell something extremely pungent. Someone gives you a piece of metal jewelry. You find a metal coin on the ground or somewhere unexpected. You see someone wearing all white or a white dog,

"Metal gives us our sense of quality and value, and our capacity to look at what lies beyond ourselves. It gives us the power to let go. It represents our father." Neil Gumenick

Five Element Angel of Wood

Characteristics: Spring, east, birth, numbers three and eight, wheat, fish, sheep, Jupiter, liver, gallbladder, 11:00 p.m.-3:00 a.m., green, shouting, rancid, kindness, anger, sour, sinuses, eyes, and wind.

Action ideas: Hug a tree. Carve some wood. Shout your excitement in a forest. Fly a kite. Look up at the sky toward Jupiter. Wear green. Give birth to an idea that's been on the back burner or in gestation period for a while. Plant flowers or give someone flowers for no reason. Enjoy sour food or put lemon/lime in your water.

Signs of Angel of Wood interaction: A giant gust of wind occurs. The wind blows something off the table or a door open. You see a fish jump out of the water or an aquarium with fish. You get a tingle or itch in your nose or a tear in your eye. You meet someone with green eyes. You see triplets or things in sets of three. You see the number eight or the infinity (∞) symbol.

"If we have followed nature's way and taken a winter rest, we too emerge into spring 'raring to go,' with clear vision and a sense of purpose. This is the season to plant seeds for a future harvest, to look ahead and make new plans, formulate new ideas, make decisions, and determine our direction for the coming year—and to take action."
Neil Gumenick

There are so many actions we can take to tap into magical energies; many are part of our daily routine, though we may not be aware yet. We can add little moments of notice and attention to these things to honor the angels of the five elements. The five elements are here to teach us and guide us to our path, healing, and aid in our journey. Nobody is alone. Take some extra time to notice the little signs in life that may be overlooked if we don't know what to pay attention to.

If you have a desire to work with a specific angel, set out time to meditate, pray, or journal with that angel. Try some of the suggestions above or make up one—you can't go wrong. Keep it simple by using the specific color of pen to write with. Or make it complicated, ornate, and intricate and use many characteristics. The most important thing is to feel good and have fun with it.

Choose something that sounds exciting and fun to you and give it a try. This can be done alone or with other people. Kids are particularly talented at easily recognizing the five element signs and five element angel signs. Go on a walk with a child and see what they notice or what kind of item they find excitement in, any animals they notice, any rocks or sticks, or a coin they pick up from the ground. Children can teach us how to notice things we may have been desensitized to or take for granted. Take your time and have fun with this!

"Only a second, that's all it takes to realize, there's a hundred thousand angels by your side. The angel personifies something new arising from the deep unconscious." Carl Jung

CHAPTER

Sixteen

The Journey Within
By Leanne Weasner

LEANNE WEASNER

Leanne Weasner is based in the Niagara Region of Canada, and spends her days as a Renal Aide in the Kidney Care Program at the SCS Hospital. She is passionate about making a difference in other people's lives. Leanne believes her most precious gifts are her empathy and compassion towards others. Leanne draws from emotional intelligence, positive psychology, and incredible confidence. Gifted with intuition, Leanne has helped many souls overcome trauma and negative life experiences. A messenger in the physical,

Leanne has the ability to connect with the spiritual realm and help those in need. Her aura shines from within and radiates the physical. Leanne may be reached at lasinspirationalquotes@outlook.com. Visit her Facebook page, L.A.s Inspirational Quotes and Healing.

Acknowledgments

Many thanks and much love to all my beautiful friends for your encouragement and support in my passion for writing. You all inspire me to live my dream and to believe in myself. Much love to all the patients in the dialysis unit for your ongoing support and love as I live my dream. You all mean so much to me and I am so grateful to be a part of your journey. A special thanks to my editor, Allyson Shaw. You are amazing and I am so grateful to have you in my life. Much love to my daughter Mikayla, you inspire me to reach for the stars. I love you with all my heart. All glory to God.

The Journey Within
By Leanne Weasner

"Some see a butterfly; some see beauty; I see heaven."

The physical and spiritual realms are separated only by belief. Believing in what you do not see is the key to all things possible. When physical and spiritual realms collide, miracles happen. Standing outside the box on this beautiful journey called life, I am blessed to see the world in a different light. As physical and spiritual realms come together, I am drawn into both. Do you believe in angels? Do you believe in a higher power? Would you believe me if I told you that you are more powerful than you think? One's soul must become completely ruined to find the spiritual map hidden deep within the physical to achieve the quest of awakening spirit.

"You must journey within to unlock your most sacred treasure—soul."

As I stood in my kitchen gazing out onto a picturesque winter scene, trees bare from cold winter days, I felt like the weather—frigid and alone. Memories fading in and out, one question repetitively playing through my mind. Knowing the sacrifices and fearing the struggle I would soon face made the answer that much more frightening. As I glanced around my beautiful home, everything I had ever wished for was surrounding me, all but me.

I always had faith in the Lord, but never knew a great deal about him. As a child, I would listen to my uncle preach every Sunday on the farm. Although I was curious to listen, my mind would mischievously wander. I knew God was someone I could turn to. I spoke to him often as a child, hoping he could hear me, but never thought he would answer. I once heard he would never leave me nor forsake me. I didn't know what that meant back then and never bothered to question.

As years passed, scars from my journey branded into my soul. I stood alone in wonder. What had I done with my life? Where was I meant to be? But the question that bothered me most was, who am I?

As I watched the snow fall lightly on the ground like feathers falling from angel's wings, I slowly began to cry. Something inside was missing. Who was I ordained to be? There is no worse feeling than knowing you are not where you are meant to be. Was I being selfish? Why was I so broken inside? As the tears flew down my cheeks, I remember quite well exactly how it went: "Dear God, are you there? It's me, I need your help. I don't know what to do. If you're there, please help me." I cradled my head in my hands, and, sobbing profusely, I leaned my elbows on the counter, burying my face into my arms. I felt numb. As the sun slowly began to shine over the bared trees, I felt a presence near. I knew I wasn't alone. As I raised my head from the countertop, eyes blurred with mascara and tears, what I saw that day would never leave me.

Standing by the steps on the main level of my home was the brightest image I had ever seen. As I stood in awe, I could feel my entire body freeze. The image stood there for mere seconds, but to me, it felt like an eternity frozen in time. I felt a calming sense of peace surround me. It was like something you would see in a movie. As the image faded quickly, I was left to second guess myself, "What just happened?" I was in complete shock! As days passed, my journey became clearer. My relationship with the Lord became one. As my faith grew, my ability to believe became unstoppable. Knowing the road ahead was going to be full of twists and turns, I did not fear because for once in my life, I knew I wasn't alone. Taking a leap of faith to conquer the quest of "Leanne Weasner" would present me with some of the most difficult challenges that would become the darkest days of my life. Yet, after battling darkness, the light within began to shine. The journey, the struggles, the scars— strength has given me the ability to believe in the stars.

"One's soul must become completely ruined to find the spiritual map hidden deep within the physical to achieve the quest of awakening spirit."

I discovered at a young age that I was blessed with challenging gifts called "empathy" and "intuition." As I became older, the gifts that I had received became a toss-up between a blessing and a curse. Having the power to feel others' emotions and to see into another's true soul became overwhelming at times, especially in close relationships. Her righteous soul danced with the devil, with unconditional love in her eyes and hope in her heart. Sometimes it felt as though I was being punished for others' pasts. It took me a long time to realize this to be a gift. Pain taught me compassion and understanding. Watching others close to my heart self-inflict pain taught me integrity. It was in my journey within that I had to learn these valuable lessons on how to disconnect from negative energy. It is a gift to be able to decipher between physical and spiritual battles. What we see in the physical is an illusion of the mind. When we translate the illusion of one's character and actions into a story of the unknown through our perceptions and experiences, we end up developing judgment. The code to unlock the mystery of another's soul is through the revelations in their eyes. Eyes tell a story, one of which the mouth cannot speak. Pain changes people; that is a fact. I am a firm believer that another's soul can only meet your energy as far as they have met their energy. When an awakened soul has found themselves in love with the presence of a soul that has not yet awakened, heartbreak will be the outcome. I have recently lived it through the battle of unrequited love. Finding true love in an empath's world is like trying to solve a fifty-year-old mystery with all the evidence in hand, but no proof. Being able to see their abilities and capabilities through the belief of the unknown is one of the greatest pains I have ever felt. Believing in someone who cannot match your frequency is one of the greatest gifts- and greatest hardships- you will ever receive. It is called unconditional love. Souls cross our path for a reason. Sometimes the reason brings pain; sometimes, the reason brings hope, most times, the reason takes a while to unfold. Everyone you meet in your journey plays a role. Having this man in my life for three years painfully revealed the woman I was ordained to be. Have you ever felt yourself in a relationship you thought was ordained by the Lord—heaven-sent? This was my belief. I was blessed to see the beauty of his soul through a spiritual level. His soul was captured between good and evil, a placement I wish to call *the drowning of a soul*. There is no right or wrong when you believe the soul crossing was meant to be. My soul simply knew. The ability to know so much about him right to the core of his pain was validation that the Lord's hand was in the meeting. When you find yourself in a relationship with a "known soul," it is for an extremely important reason.

"Her righteous soul danced with the devil,
with unconditional love in her eyes and hope in her heart."

One's soul revolves around truth. Truth equals character. Truth is hard to handle for those who look in the mirror and see beauty in their lies. When you take a huge step back and assess a situation or relationship, truth will always reveal the depth of one's soul. Having the ability to see what I am blessed to see in another's soul allows me to know the struggles, hardship, and pain they have endured. When a soul resorts to lying and deceit to save face in life, damage to another will always occur. When a true connection develops through energy in physical beings, that energy between them never dies spiritually. It is written in the word that truth is the way to righteousness. Having a clean soul does not come easy. When life gets in the way and pain suppresses the soul, it overflows with darkness. It all defaults back to the mind. The mind is extremely powerful. What we choose to absorb reflects our actions. Triggers will always haunt the mind when one's soul is not at peace. Until you are willing to go deep within to heal your soul from past traumas, pain will always cloud the light of truth. To become authentic in your journey, you must be able to look in the mirror of truth and see the light within shining back at you. Your given right is truth; thou shall be able to speak it and live it. You possess the power within to conquer the mission to live righteously.

"The truth is hard to handle for those who look in the
mirror and see beauty in their lies."

Believing in what we do not see is the answer. If you
look back on your life, would you be able to see how things
meant for you had a mysterious way of aligning, and things
meant to teach you ended in pain? Pain equals knowledge. If
I had a dollar for every time I was called crazy for the way I
spoke and thought, I would be retired, living on an island
sipping margaritas as I laugh to myself. This too is a gift.
Being able to see the spiritual realm is one of the most
amazing gifts I have received from the Lord. Looking out on
this beautiful world, I see God everywhere. He is in you and
in me. His presence is in nature and in all things beautiful.
One thing I have learned in my journey is: God is love. The
heart is the most valuable treasure to the soul. The heart, the
mind, and the soul are oneness. It is who you are. We are
spiritual beings living a human experience. We are here to
learn, to teach, but most of all, to love. Love will always
guide your soul when your intentions in mind are pure. The
soul knows its way home; to unlock the mystery of the mind
you must feel from the heart. Knowing who you are is half
the battle in discovering your soul. Believing is key to
unlocking the mystery of knowing there is a great deal more
out there. Some see a butterfly; some see beauty; I see
heaven. Have you ever had certain things happen to you that
you could not explain? Have you ever seen a butterfly and
felt a presence near? Have you ever found a dime and a loved
one that has passed crossed your mind? Signs. Signs are
everywhere when you have awakened to the beauty the
universe holds. Have you ever heard the phrase, "Ask, and
you shall receive"? Power is within. Your mind can create

the impossible. We are given dreams and visions for a reason. They hold the key to our heart's desires. We are here on a mission. Each unique in our individual way. The heart holds the power to believe, while the mind holds the power to conquer. Finding your true path in life comes from within. Everything you have gone through in life plays a role in who you are meant to be—the greater the struggle, the bigger the blessing.

"The journey, the struggles, the scars. Strength has given her the ability to believe in the stars."

I am blessed to help many souls that cross my path in need. Intuition comes from the heart and speaks from the core. When I am in the presence of a soul in need, God speaks. My heart rate goes into overdrive, and the messages come to mind. I do not consider myself to be psychic, I am merely a messenger on a mission to help those in need. The reward does not come in the form of monetary value; the reward is far greater—believers. The power you possess is waiting within. You must journey within to unlock your most sacred treasure— your soul. Through meditation, exercise, nature, and self-care, you can achieve a spiritual connection. You must become one with the universe and go deep within. You must know who you are and the beauty you possess. Believing is the key that will set your soul free. Becoming comfortable with being uncomfortable will push you out of your comfort zone to reach for the stars. You were born to shine, blessed with life. You are a spiritual being blessed with many gifts to achieve your quest. No matter what your role in life, always believe you are exactly where you are meant to be, right on time. Do you believe me when I say you are more powerful than you think? Do you believe in angels? I do because one just gave this message to you. The spiritual realm is waiting for you, are you ready?

"Soul knows its way home, to unlock the mystery of the mind you must feel from the heart."

CHAPTER

Seventeen

My Angelic Encounter
By Misty Proffitt-Thompson

MISTY PROFFITT-THOMPSON

Misty Thompson is a spiritual life coach, a mind, body, and spirit practitioner, an author, teacher, and speaker. Her passion is to help those who are struggling with their connection to source because of the grief they carry. Misty lives in Thatcher, Arizona, has four children and four grandchildren. To learn more, go to www.mistymthompson.com.

My Angelic Encounter
By Misty Proffitt-Thompson

Receiving an angelic encounter took me completely by surprise. I have heard stories of others being fortunate with this incredible honor, but when I experienced my meeting, I received validation that these amazingly beautiful messengers of God are real.

If you are someone who wants to have a personal experience, I will describe to you how it happened to me, why I received their message, and what you can do that will guide you toward receiving inspiring messages from the angels.

One of my mentors helped me become familiar with communicating with the angels. The key is to be open to the possibilities. When you begin to question, analyze, or think too much about what the message will be, when you will receive it, if you will receive it, and how it will show up, you will find that you will not obtain your guidance. Once you begin to question, it means that you are bringing the mind into the equation, not to mention the ego. That is a recipe for sabotaging yourself. Keep in mind, the message may still be sent; however, you will be analyzing too much and will no doubt miss the golden opportunity.

My sister died back in 1993, and I continually felt a connection to her at night when I laid in bed. It was as though I would be able to respond should someone come into my room and talk to me, yet at the same time, I was entering a dream-like state. The messages that I received were guidance, but I didn't understand it at that time. Fast forward to January 2016, I was in the process of starting my first book, *By Your Side: A Journey of Two Sisters through Love and Sacrifice*, where I talked about the circumstances surrounding my sister's death and the encounters I had, and I went to bed envisioning what this project would look like and what the book title should be. I laid down and sunk into my bed, resting my head on my pillow, still fantasizing about my book. I felt that this would be so incredibly easy. As I lay there, I began to feel overwhelmed with the title. I wanted a title that would capture the essence of my sister and I working together from our beginning, specifically, her in spirit and me in the physical sense.

I began to fall deeper into sleep while my body became heavier and heavier, and like I had experienced in 1993 before the encounter with my sister, I felt as though I was drifting deeper into my trance-like state. As I lay on my right side, I felt a lull between the mattress and my side, right above my hip. I thought that this lull was my daughter trying so desperately to slide her arm around my waist to hug me. I woke, slightly, and turned my head, but no one was there. I felt an invisible energetic arm surround my entire upper body. It reminded me of a warm electric blanket, but it wasn't touching me. I felt as though I was swaddled in loving warmth. That was when I felt chills start at the top of my head and race down my body. These chills weren't associated with being cold; these chills were warm. I felt an incredible amount of peace with these chills, and I was safe. Knowing that this was complete unconditional love and safety, I knew it was an encounter from one of God's messengers.

The warmth and safety of my guardian angel stayed with me for a few additional minutes, and when I felt it leave me, I was saddened, but at the same time, appreciative. Receiving such a message allowed me to believe that I have a connection with the spiritual realm.

I continue to have a connection to the angels; however, I have not obtained the guidance like I did that day. I am open to whatever messages that the angels provide to me, and I do receive feathers, coincidences, and validations through meditation that I know are from my angels. As much as I would love to have the experience of my guardian angel surround me with unconditional love again, I know that it isn't necessary because as much as I am open to it, that experience impacted me in a way that will stay with me forever, so there is no need to have that experience recreated.

To connect with your angels, there are a few steps to follow:

1. You must believe it is possible. To have doubt will almost ensure that it will not happen. As humans, we tend to dismiss anything that we cannot see with our eyes, or we believe that it is possible for others to have those experiences, but we downplay the fact that we are deserving as well.

2. Believe that you are deserving. You deserve and are as worthy of having a connection to your angels as the next person. We are all here in this physical sense because we are children of God; therefore, we are all worthy.

3. Asking for help is necessary because we have free will. This is a huge blessing, but it is also a huge

responsibility where we must be accountable for the choices that we make. Ultimately, it is our choice to ask for help. Asking gives the angels permission to assist us, and we must be clear and specific on what we are asking for. This does not mean we will get exactly what we are asking for, but if we are clear on what we are asking for, there will be no room for the misinterpretation. The assistance we receive is always for the good and higher purpose for all of those who are affected. Sometimes our choices may affect beyond us, and we must be mindful of that.

4. We must choose to trust the guidance and be open to receive the message without manipulating the results that you are needing or wanting. Showing complete faith in God and his messengers is a testament of how greatly we trust that divine guidance. Surrendering control can be difficult, but that is what makes the received message so appreciated, creditable, and will strengthen your faith. The more you witness that faith, the bigger it will grow.

The angels will connect with you and for you in a way that is meaningful to you. Some of the ways I have experienced and/or heard about from my clients include hearing a specific song on the radio, seeing feathers or coins, smelling certain smells, and witnessing a certain image that is not common from two different sources. I assure you that if you begin to analyze the message, you will no longer receive it. These encounters do occur more than you realize. Think back to a time when you connected with a stranger who happened to say the exact thing you needed to hear. Possibly you thought of someone from your past, and you ran into them unexpectedly. Some may call those "coincidences." Coincidences are merely those chance experiences that are brought on by the divine.

Here are some tips to follow that will strengthen and establish your belief in messages from the angels:

1. Follow a daily routine of prayer or meditation to connect to inner divine guidance. During this time, ask and be being specific on what you need help, with but keep the *how* out of the equation.

2. Keep a journal around you during the day. Write the date along with the experiences that you believe are serendipitous or coincidental which you encounter, even if it doesn't make sense at the time. Trust that it is a message that will reveal itself when the time is right.

3. Write down any dreams that you may have that involve a loved one (who has passed away or is still alive), angels, or any other divine presence.

4. Show gratitude and appreciation once you have asked for assistance and when you believe you have received guidance. Being grateful for the angels, for God, and the experiences to help you with the higher good will ensure that you will draw those kinds of occurrences to you.

Your connection and encounter will more than likely be different than my experience and that is the beauty of it—it is a personal relationship that is tailored for you. As you become skilled in being open to receive, trust, believe, and ask for guidance, then you can ensure that you, too, will have an incredible angelic experience that will change you forever.

CHAPTER

Eighteen

Everything Will Be
Alright Next Time
By Rosemary Hurwitz

ROSEMARY HURWITZ

Rosemary Hurwitz, a married mom of four young adults, is passionate about an inner-directed life, and she found the focus for it in the Enneagram. The Enneagram is a time-honored personality-to-higher-consciousness paradigm used worldwide. An accredited professional member of the International Enneagram Association, Rosemary has been on the faculty at Common Ground in Chicago since 2010, and has been published in five inspirational compilation books, including *No Mistakes, How You Can Change*

Adversity into Abundance. Her first single-authored best-selling book is *Who You Are Meant To Be, The Enneagram Effect*. She received her Enneagram Certification in 2001, through an MA. Pastoral Studies program at Loyola University in Chicago, Illinois. Rosemary coaches with and teaches the Enneagram internationally.

Acknowledgments

Thank you to Dr. John Bond and Dr. Donna Amstutz for guiding me to my deeper self.

Everything Will Be Alright Next Time
By Rosemary Hurwitz

This is a story of hope and faith.

When I was 33, my husband and I lost our pregnancy, and our baby, at 21-and-a-half weeks. I held her and kissed her goodbye on her small and incredibly sweet forehead.

I held her and grieved, and I did not spend a long time with her that morning of September 3rd in the hospital. I remember saying calmly, after holding her for a few minutes, "Please take her back, because I cannot have her."

We named her Kelly Marie. Kelly means warrior, and Marie was for Mary, the mother of Jesus. Somehow Mary was with me throughout this test of faith, and this baby had been a fighter throughout a pregnancy that was not right from the start.

I remember going to the doctor for my check-up one day. There was a woman who chatted with me. She was sitting alone in the waiting room, and looked at me with great empathy after I told her my story of spotting that was starting and stopping, no matter how much lying down I did. She prophetically asked me, "Have you prepared yourself for the worst?" A perennial optimist, I said, "I feel hopeful and do not like to worry."

When I went into the hospital at approximately five months into the pregnancy, I was filled with hope and faith that I would return like I had the first time I was pregnant. I would bring home a beautiful baby. I knew I would be on bed rest, but I was hopeful. I had Placenta Previa, which was a condition that worked out with a baby going to full term about 50 percent of the time.

At 20 weeks of pregnancy, I went into the hospital, and at 21-and-a-half weeks, I came home. With no rhyme or reason, they said, I would alternately bleed and stop bleeding. It was mostly the Braxton Hicks contractions that were slowly pulling the placenta off of its wall. Eventually, my placenta would abrupt in the middle of the night at the hospital. As my womb grew larger, it couldn't hold in place, and it was too soon. As a large piece of it flew out of me in the middle of the night, the nurses rushed in, and my doctor was soon there by my side telling me I was in shock.

I asked if I could have a C-section, because I read about a baby boy in People magazine who had been delivered by C-section. He had been born blind at 22 weeks, but was a miracle. I wanted a miracle. They did perform a C-section, but only after they switched horses midstream, so to speak. The bleeding was so bad that a C-section was the only option.

The doctor came in to see me after I woke up, and said, "Your baby girl didn't make it." He told me about the necessary C-section that I was put under for. I was always glad, even in my deepest grief, that I had asked for a C-section, even though I cried so hard to my sister about not getting anything for it, because it made me realize the strength of a mother's love. Our baby went to her heavenly home, and I had so much anger at God, I felt I would die too.

One night, when my Jewish husband said our Christian blessing at dinner, as we had been teaching our daughter to do, I said, "I don't want to pray." He responded with, "You don't have to, but we are only blessing our food."

Ultimately, we loved each other through this time of grief. My husband was my rock, accepting how intensely wounded I felt, while minimizing his grief. With a social worker the hospital recommended, we would work on both expressing the grief in our individual ways. The therapist told my husband, "You can't be over it this soon."

Our two-year-old daughter, Claire, helped me to keep my feet on the ground, as did an excellent therapist, who helped me through the grief and loss of a baby who was wanted and loved so much already.

After the physical wounds of the surgery were beginning to heal, a good deal of the outside support I received had faded away, and my mother had gone home, I started to genuinely experience the grief. It was so severe that I thought I would not make it. I cried so much and felt so drained, and I did not want to frighten my daughter. My dear sister-in-law sent me a beautiful book called *Ended Beginnings*, from which I received comfort.

One day, my daughter, who was still a baby herself at only two years of age, caught me staring into space. She sweetly said, "I miss you, Mommy." I hugged her and cried more, and then did my best to pull myself together for her sake. It was then that I realized that I needed more consistent support. Every few weeks, with the social worker's guidance, my husband and I worked on our communication and acceptance of the different ways people grieve. I needed some help to get through the darkness in my world. The therapist helped me and let me express my anger and hate at the world—at God—in a safe space.

In the initial six weeks of therapy, I was unable to sleep when my little girl took her naps, although I always felt exhausted. But one mid-October day, as she napped, something shifted in the grief process. The warm sun poured through my living room window onto the couch where I rested, and this serene and glowing light relaxed my body into a peaceful sleep.

The bright light enveloped me, and as I slept, I dreamed of a bright, white light that was intensely beautiful. In that illuminating light, which was so awesome and filled the entire screen of my mind, Mary, the mother of Jesus, appeared. She was standing within it, and when I woke up, I knew in my heart and have always known with a deep certainty, that it was her. I heard her say two things to me. I will never forget them. "Everything will be all right next time. There will be a boy."

I woke up, feeling rested and peaceful for the first time in the several weeks after we had said goodbye to our baby, Kelly Marie.

Not knowing for sure if it was merely a dream, or a visit from this dearest of angels, I talked it over with my therapist. She helped me look into my heart, and I knew it came from deep within me, was real, and was a gift from Mary to help and comfort me.

The following June, as life blossomed around us, we found we were pregnant again. I shared with my husband what I heard in the dream—what Mary had said to me. She was a messenger of God's hope to me, of that I was certain, and my intuition felt as if it was on fire! My husband encouraged me to hang onto her message with all of my might through the anxiety of a subsequent pregnancy. I continued in therapy, so I would be able to more easily let go of any of the normal and often irrational fears that might happen to a pregnant woman after a loss.

This new pregnancy was healthy and easy, and again, we chose not to know the sex of the baby ahead of time. I would have moments where I would get anxiety, but the doctor and the therapist reassured me that it was about the subsequent pregnancy and was normal after trauma. I managed it to the best of my ability, with help, so as not to affect the new baby coming.

In March of the following year, nine months later, my doctor came in and said I would need to have a C-section, as they were concerned the extended labor that I was in, if left to go on too long, could leave our baby in distress. I was extremely scared, and cried out that I did not want to have a C-section, that it would remind me of the crises in the hospital in the middle of the night when we lost the baby.

The doctor asked me if I had any control over when I got my period. I said, "No." She assured me that I did not have control over when a baby comes either, and told me to do my best to breathe and relax in knowing that I was the vessel, and did not have control over how and when this baby came.

I realized what she was saying was true; I was not in control of something as big as birth. She said, "I will give you 15 more minutes, and then we will have to deliver this baby." That peace was all that I needed, because she came back to check on me and said, "You are dilated to nine centimeters—you can push—let's go!"

Within minutes, our son, Christopher, was born. We all cried with relief along with this big healthy nine pound, ten ounce newborn baby boy who made his way into the world, helping me heal.

"Everything will be all right next time. There will be a boy." These words of hope echoed through me, and my entire body trembled and it would not—could not—stop. I shivered relentlessly until this baby latched onto me and took his first drink, and a calm humility came over me. I was no longer interested in controlling everything in God's world, but only being a servant to what was meant to be for me. It was a knowing that was both deeply clear and not fully understood. I was finally in acceptance, the final stage of grief, according to Elizabeth Kubler-Ross, author of *On Death And Dying* (1969.)

The birth of one baby and loss of another is a mystery, but even now, with our baby boy grown into a beautiful young man and father of his own little boy, I hold onto the huge feelings of faith that I found in the moment of his birth. When I met him and fed him, and felt Mary's arms wrapped around us both, I experienced a re-birth—a connection to my spirit that was profound.

I knew deep within my soul that the message I received from the divine realm was true. And I knew with every part of me that everything is right in God's world.

CHAPTER

Ninteen

My Connection To Angels
By Sue Broome

SUE BROOME

Sue Broome, a gifted intuitive healer, spiritual teacher and international best-selling author, works with the divine and angels in guiding others on their spiritual healing journey. Each session or workshop leaves you feeling empowered. She loves teaching how to connect with their loved ones through her book, *Signs From Your Loved Ones*, and courses: *Memories Shared with your Loved Ones*, and

Channel Writing with Mom. Our loved ones want to connect. She created *The Desert Speaks* oracle deck, which can be used for inspiration and readings for yourself and others. Her latest book, *The Experience Book, 21 Days of Beautiful Experiences from the Angels*, will allow so many to be filled with joy, love, peace, and harmony, as the angels remind us so often. Enjoy *Healing Tools From the Angels*, a free PDF for you: Empowerment4You.com/angel-talk-with-sue.

Acknowledgments

I would like to express my gratitude to all of the angels who have encouraged me on my spiritual journey, many who are here in physical form, and many who are in spirit. I have learned so much along the way, and am grateful to be able to share this wisdom with others. My heart is open to the inspiration and assistance I receive each and every day from the divine and the angels, both human and spirit. Thank you all who have allowed me into your lives, to share this knowledge, and offer tools of empowerment for your spiritual journey. And thank you to publishers, such as Kyra Schaefer and As You Wish Publishing, for an outlet to share the inspiration and words of angels to encourage and help others.

My Connection To Angels
By Sue Broome

Growing up, I don't recall angels ever being a topic of discussion at home. Despite going to churches regularly, both Catholic and Lutheran, and attending parochial school from first through eighth grades, I have no recollection of angels being taught or spoken of.

Thinking back, I find that rather strange, as angels are found in many religions in some way, shape, or form. Angels are not tied to any one religion, and many people consider themselves spiritual and not religious. That definitely describes me—spiritual.

It wasn't until I was well into my 30s that I met anyone who talked about angels. When I heard about them, this opened me up to becoming curious, and I started reading. I would search out almost any book I could find that was about angels.

I read other people's stories about how angels had appeared to them and helped them with an illness, or how they were close to being in an accident that would surely have taken their life had angels not intervened. There were stories of people who experienced miracles in their lives, and these people attributed them to angels.

There were stories of people who were connecting with angels or meeting their guardian angels. These were the stories that truly intrigued me. I wanted to learn about this "connecting with angels" and how to do it. I wanted to have a connection with angels. I wanted to meet my angels; I wanted to know how to invite them into my life.

I started with additional reading. At the time, it seemed like that was all there was—various books about angels. I loved going to the bookstore, grabbing a stack of books, hanging out at the coffee shop, and deciding which ones to take home.

What I discovered in all of my reading, was that the angels, our guardian angels and the archangels, *want* to connect and work with us too! They want to help us throughout our day. They are happy to assist us. In fact, they are waiting for us to invite them into our lives.

As I started connecting and working with the angels, both the right people and the right classes started showing up in my life at exactly the right time. Before I knew it, I was doing readings and healing work. To be exact, the angels were doing the healing work and guiding me in those readings. I was now the interpreter between the angels and my clients.

Over the years in working with clients and holding workshops, the question that seems to have come up the most is the question I started with: "How do I connect with the angels?"

How do I connect with the angels?

Over time, I discovered the more I connected with the angels, the more I was able to connect automatically. What I mean is that initially, it started out as a ritual that was basically a step-by-step process. Yet, the more I followed this initial process, the more streamlined and automatic it became to connect. Before long, I knew and truly felt deep within that, in fact, I was always connected to the angels— that the angels were always with me.

Clients often ask me, "How can I connect?" They don't generally ask me, "Why would I want to connect?" They have usually already heard enough about angels to know what their *why* is, and this *why* is extremely personal and unique to each person.

Here's a funny story that happened recently. I was talking with someone who didn't truly believe in angels (though I'd seen glimpses of hope), and they needed assistance with an issue in their life. As we were about to hang up from our phone call, I said, "I will get the angels on it." That was all I said. Later that day—I'm talking hours— I received a text from this person that read: "Your angels work fast." They had received exactly what they needed, they took the necessary action, and now everything was back on track. I merely chuckled and thanked the angels for their help.

I want to point out, however, that they are not *my* angels. The angels are here for all of us.

The easiest way I know of to work with the angels is to *ask.* Yes, ask. There you have it. All the guidance from the books I've read over the years boils down to those three letters.

Okay, that is the super-condensed version of my years of reading and experience. If you wish to get connected to the angels, I can start you out with a step-by-step process, and before long, you will discover your personal streamlined way of working with them.

Step-by-step connecting to angels

The first time you do this process, you may want your intention simply to be to connect with the angels, so you can get to know the feeling of an angelic presence. This is an easy process, although we as humans tend to overthink and overcomplicate things far too much. I excel at the skill of overthinking.

I have found that creating your space is important. It does not need to be the same location every single time, though for some that may work better. I do recommend, however, that the space you choose is quiet, without outside distractions, and is a place where you feel safe. When I use the word *safe*, what I'm referring to is a place where you feel comfortable closing your eyes. I don't want you to feel like you have to open one eye every time you hear a sound. Also, this is to be a space where if you do happen to fall asleep, you'll feel okay in your surroundings.

You'll want a comfortable place to sit. You may choose to lie down, although I recommend the first few times that you sit.

You may want to light a candle, though that is not necessary. You may want to have a journal nearby for any impressions or thoughts that come to you, so that you can jot them down. This is entirely up to you. The more you do this process and connect with the angels, the better you will become at knowing what works best for you.

Some of you may even want to have soft music playing, though again, this is not necessary.

I would also like to mention that imagination and visualization do play a part in this process. If you feel you cannot visualize or have no imagination, let me give you this quick example. I would like you to visualize or imagine a lemon. I am certain a picture of a lemon has now popped into your mind. I bring this up because when I was first connecting with the angels, I would discount my imagination and didn't feel I could visualize. Time and time again, however, images, thoughts, and/or feelings would all come forward.

Your intention is to connect with an angel. Whenever you are working with angels, you need to ask for what you would like. You could say something like, "Angels, I invite you to connect with me during this meditation." Change the words to what feels right for you. You may speak them out loud, think of them in your mind, or write the words in your journal. Do whatever feels right for you. You may want to try this out in different ways and see what you notice.

Hold the intention of connecting with an angel in your mind and in your heart. And again, you may also want to say it out loud, though it is not necessary. So, let's begin:

- Sit comfortably with your feet on the floor.

- Close your eyes and place your hand over your heart.

- Take a deep breath, breathing in through your nose and out through your mouth.

- Take several additional deep breaths.

- Allow your body to relax a bit with each breath, allowing any doubts or expectations to float away each time you exhale. Notice how your breathing slows down a little the more relaxed you get.

• Imagine you are sitting at the beach. You are under an umbrella, and there is a gentle ocean breeze you can feel on your skin. The only sounds you hear are those of the waves lapping at the shore and the cry of seagulls. You notice the smell of salt in the air. It feels refreshing and cleansing, as well as calming.

• Take another deep breath, allowing your body to get even more relaxed.

• Focus on the rhythm of the waves lapping on the beach. Hear them as they come in and wash back out again.

• Soon you get the sense that someone is walking toward you. Your eyes are still closed, and you are feeling so relaxed and calm, you don't want to open them. So, you simply notice. You realize they are sitting next to you under the umbrella. You feel comfortable and safe, so you still do not feel a need to open your eyes. You continue to focus on the sound of the waves and the smell of the salty air.

• Notice what you are feeling, besides being calm and safe. Notice anything coming up without trying to change anything. Just notice.

• Continue to sit quietly, smelling the fresh ocean breeze.

• Feel them taking your hand and gently holding it between both of theirs.

- Their hands feel soft, and it's almost as if you can feel the love emanating from their palms.

- They place something in your palm. It doesn't feel like anything you've ever felt before. They whisper, "Hold this to your heart and allow it to melt into your true essence."

- Place your palm to your heart, and as soon as you do, whatever was placed in your hand dissipates. Imagine the warm feeling of loving energy flowing, starting at your heart to encompass your entire being. Allow your cells to absorb the love. Bask in this wonderful feeling for as long as you would like.

- Take a few deep breaths, allowing this loving feeling to continue.

- You sense they are no longer beside you, and you slowly open your eyes. As you glance down the beach, you see what could only be an angel, walking along right where the water meets the sand. Their head turns as you see them and your eyes meet. The loving embrace you feel from catching their glance only confirms what you already know in your heart. It was an angel.

- Thank them for the wonderful gift.

If you didn't feel exactly the way described, that's okay. Everyone has a unique experience, and each time you do the process, you may feel something different. Allowing your experience to be what it is, without any expectation, is important.

If, for some reason, you did not feel anything, do this process several times over the next few days, allowing your experience to unfold.

This is a simple, yet powerful, process of connecting with an angel. Here are some thoughts you may want to journal about:

- Notice the feelings you had during the process and afterward.

- When you placed the angel gift into your heart, what did you feel?

- What did you sense as they were sitting next to you?

- Were there any colors, scents, sounds, or memories you noticed?

You may want to have a special journal for all of your angelic connections.

Daily connections to angels and archangels

Once you've connected a few times, and recognize the feeling of the angel, continue inviting them into your day. Start out your day by inviting them to be with you throughout the entire day. You don't need any special words, but remember to ask and thank them for any assistance they may offer.

Here are a few ideas for you, using the same process, and setting different intentions:

- Ask the angel for their name. You may receive a name instantly, or you may softly hear a name or phrase. Then, over the next day or so, you may hear the same phrase or name several times as a confirmation.

• Ask for some guidance regarding a specific topic. Your guidance may come in sounds, colors, words, feelings, or thoughts that may seem like they are yours. Ideas may seem to pop into your mind out of nowhere, or perhaps you will experience synchronicities. All of these may come into play. Journaling is helpful to sort them all out.

• Ask an archangel to connect, and notice how the energy of each one is unique and feels different from others. Here are a few archangels to call upon and invite into your day and your life:

  • Archangel Michael for strength, courage, and feeling safe.

  • Archangel Raphael for healing and help with relationships.

  • Archangel Gabriel for communication when speaking, writing, or creating in any way.

No matter which angels you are working with, thank them for the wonderful gift of whatever information or healing you may have received from them.

The angels are here for everyone. They want to help you throughout your day. They want to become an automatic go-to for everything that comes up in your life, from the smallest of topics to larger decisions. The more you work with the angels, inviting them into your day, the more you will notice them in your day.

I invite the angels into my day each and every morning. I find myself saying, "Thank you," out loud, automatically, throughout my day. I know they are there whether I'm going for a walk in the morning, working with a client, or resting my head for the night. They are with me.

Two of my favorite sayings are still,

"Calling all angels," and "Angels, angels, everywhere." There are definitely specialty angels, although if you aren't certain which angel is for what, that's okay.

Repeat after me: "Calling all angels." "Angels, angels everywhere." "Thank you, angels." You have covered all the bases.

This process may sound almost too easy to do anything. The angels want us to connect with them, so they want the process to be as easy as possible. As I said in the beginning, the more you connect with the angels, it will start to become automatic, and before long, you will know you are always connected.

I cannot imagine my life without angels. With expanded love coming into Mother Earth from the angelic realm and beyond, increasing numbers of people want to know how to have their individual connection to the angels. I do hope this process is a wonderful starting point for your personal connection. If you have been working with the angels for a long time, I hope you also have found this simple process beneficial. Angel blessings to you.

CHAPTER

Twenty

I Believe In Angels
By Suzanne Harmony

SUZANNE HARMONY

Suzanne Harmony is an author, teacher, psychic, and medium. She established Harmony House Healing Center in 2004. She is a dedicated and fun-loving grandmother, who lives in North Bay, Ontario, Canada with Dr. Mario Lemay. An epiphany led Harmony to write, *Leap of Faith...From Fear to Fulfillment* (2008). This inspirational book empowers readers to grow in self-awareness and acceptance of their uniqueness. Her self-help memoir, *Because I Didn't Tell*, (2017) with pen name, I. Katchastarr, details her account of the horrific events of her young adult life that fiercely unraveled her once safe world. Two gems found at the end of each chapter serve to soothe readers: self-forgiveness and pearls of wisdom. An As You Wish published author, Harmony has collaborated with other authors in: *Inspirations* and *When Angels Speak*. Her solo-authored *WTF (Willing To Forgive)* workbook will be available soon. You can reach Suzanne Harmony at www.HarmonyHelps.ca.

Acknowledgments

I have been blessed with loving support throughout my life, and for these people I am especially grateful: My dear parents, Ray and June Pigeon, Dr. Mario Lemay and our children—your enthusiasm, loyalty, compassion, and patience keeps me focused. Kyra and Todd Schaefer, my delightful publishers and encouragement champs—you have made writing, podcasting, and getting published a breeze. Liz Dawn Donahue and Sunny Dawn Johnston, thank you for strengthening my presentation skills through your Celebrate Your Life (CYL) Online Speakers Training Program. My volunteer work scholarship at CYL Events has blessed me with "my soul tribe," and beautiful connections. My loyal friends, clients, students, community organizations, radio and television interviewers, who have welcomed me with my passionate purpose into your world, thank you for your openness and love. Readers everywhere, thank you for choosing this book and exploring my work.

I Believe In Angels
By Suzanne Harmony

I truly do believe in angels, and I have chosen to celebrate their gracious presence in my life by dedicating this chapter to the miracles that I have experienced, the fears that I have overcome, the hurdles I have jumped, and the blessings I live with every day thanks to the angels in my life.

Any time that I have been faced with doubt, I take a moment to sit quietly and remind myself to call upon the angels for assistance. When I do call them, they immediately arrive. Their calming presence allows me to trust their sincere desire to be of assistance, and that they indeed have come to my rescue.

You have the same access to the angels. When you sincerely wish to communicate with them, simply calm your mind, find a quiet and safe place to relax, close your eyes, take a few long, slow deep breaths, and ask the angels to guide you. Even when you are not so relaxed, when you need them, simply call out, "Angels, help!" and they will come. Trust their guidance; do not presume anything. Their guidance, words, or solution *is* what's best for you.

Angels, spirit guides, animal guides, and divine helpers of all kinds have created a definite upswing in my life. They have given me faith, clarity, and confidence to move forward fearlessly. I trust these shared experiences will help you to believe in angels and truly hear when angels speak.

My first significant and most powerful leap of faith was brought on by my trust in the angel voice of Grace. She came to me when I was fearful for my life and the lives of my children, and wondering how I could save us. Grace whispered this freeing segment of the Catholic vow of marriage to me: "What God has brought together, no man shall tear apart." Our marriage was certainly not "God-given." I was threatened to do so with his gun pointed to my head.

It was after the birth of our twins, Chantal and Chad. Chad, miraculously, chose to be an angel, as he died upon his delivery. What a blessing you are, Chad, to have chosen to allow your two sisters and me to move forward in our life; knowing, my dear Chad, that had you survived, the next chapter of our lives would probably have been filled with more grief than if you had survived. Not because of you—because of the troubled man who "fathered" the three of you. This leap of faith required that I leave him. It's as if Chad, a true angel in our lives, knew that had he survived, perhaps this sick man would not have fallen out of our lives. A son is what he truly desired, and he certainly would have behaved differently in a fight for custody of his son. Although it was with disgrace, and after an emotionally disturbing battle, he did choose to leave us alone.

I, like many parents, would die to save my children! I am forever grateful for Grace, that I live to tell this truth, and that we now live joyful, fulfilling experiences and are blessed with true love!

Another angelically-guided moment that I experienced occurred when I set out to meditate in my favorite peaceful, secret-hideaway location in the forest that hugs Duchesne Falls. I took a much-needed time-out from my busy schedule, and chose to embrace this beautiful, sunshine-kissed spring day with a hearty hike up the falls to quiet my busy mind, breathe in the fresh, clean air, and take time to count my many blessings. I unwrinkled the blanket as I spread it out onto the rock clearing in the woods, off the well-traveled path that laced the thundering falls. Then, I made myself comfortable on it as I prepared to meditate. Before I surrendered to this peaceful practice, I thanked God for this glorious day, and I asked God and the angels to protect me during this respite. The rhythmic rumbling of the falls, as the spring thaw spilled over and splashed up against the rocks, naturally quieted my noisy mind, and the cheerful chirping of the birds made my heart sing. I smiled as I easily fell into deep meditation. I welcomed the new warmth of the spring sun and decided to remove some clothing, feeling safe and secure in this peaceful, secret setting, surrounded by God's great creation. I confidently lay back down on the blanket. The sun warmed me and softly kissed my winter white skin; for this, too, I was grateful.

I was quite relaxed in this blissful state of being when suddenly, the wind changed. The gentle, warm breeze turned sharp and cold. It sparked my awareness, and I accepted this as a sign. I then heard the familiar voice of Grace, as she prompted me to "Get dressed, get up, and prepare to leave," which I did, calmly and confidently, and I thanked Grace for her guidance. Just as I stepped away from this special place, I realized that I had forgotten my sunglasses. I turned around to pick them up, only to see, that coming toward me along the path, was a gentleman. I stepped out of sight and watched him walk joyfully down the path beside the falls. I picked up my sunglasses, and once again thanked Grace, God, and the angels for protecting me and keeping me safe. I continued along the path that brought me to the bridge on the highway that covers the falls. I glanced down at the gravel in front of me, and there before my eyes, was a small brass crucifix. I picked it up, and upon examining it, I noticed that above the figure of Jesus nailed to the cross was a beautifully engraved rose, not the usual Latin scroll of "INHS." I turned it over to see what else this interesting treasure had to offer me, and in pure delight and amazement, I read the delicately engraved words: "God Protect." Wow! Tears came easily to my eyes as I glanced to the heavens above and, once again, I thanked God and Grace, the angels and nature's magic for their divine protection, and especially for this miraculous confirmation of their constant presence and protective service. I carry this crucifix with me, and I delight in recounting this amazing story whenever I show it to people who are interested in hearing about the living truth, my experiences and my belief in angels.

Angels channel messages through me for the clients I treat with Reiki, some of whom have ascended to heaven. Prior to their death, they trusted and always encouraged me to tell them all of what was revealed to me about their health, their condition, their progress, and the angel messages. One beautiful young lady, experiencing leukemia for the second time in her short life, thanked me for bringing her to a peaceful, pain-free state and for always being honest with her. She, with joyful conviction, guaranteed me that she would visit Harmony House frequently, in spirit form, after her surrender to cancer. She has followed through with that promise. I know it's her presence when I repeatedly hit the *off* button on the reception room stereo before I leave for the night and it won't turn off. I quickly realize her presence, surrender to the humor of it all, and agree to let her listen to the music for as long as she desires. I am never surprised to notice that it is off when I return to Harmony House the following day. On another occasion, I was standing in front of the bathroom mirror, putting on my make-up and preparing for my first client of the day. I was thinking about this delightful young client who now visits Harmony House in spirit form and how fortunate I am to experience her presence and her humor, when suddenly a whole roll of toilet paper completely unraveled and gathered in a layered pile at my feet. I laughed with delight and thanked Stephanie for her powerful, playful presence. She also delights in making the lights flicker, opening the creakiest basement door, and creating the sound of someone first sitting down in the wicker rocking chair, when there's actually no one in it! She certainly keeps me entertained, and I am forever grateful for her cheerful, spiritual presence.

Many clients who open themselves up to experience all that is available to them during their session receive confirmation of their deceased loved ones' actual cause of death, their present state of being, their messages to the client, and much more. I am always impressed by the signs that they give me to share with the client. These signs confirm exactly who is communicating with them. They will show up in an outfit that only the client would remember, or raise a glass of their favorite beverage in greetings to the client—much like they would do in real life. Some of them come with the scent of their favorite perfume, knowing that my client would also remember that about their loved one. Some share verbal expressions in the exact words that my client is familiar with. All of this is emotionally gratifying and reassuring to my clients. I am truly blessed to share this gift and honored to have been chosen to do so. I believed for the longest time that these angelic visits, messages, and events were a blessing to clients during Reiki sessions, and would only occur at Harmony House. As I pondered this, I began to receive messages everywhere, at any time, and for people I had not even met yet! Wow!

During an uplifting presentation to 33 yoga students in another city, I was able to deliver personalized messages to each participant. This happens with every presentation now.

Recently, I was preparing myself for the day, when I received angel messages for my dear friend, Anne Danielle. I am always delighted when angels speak to me out of the blue like this. I trust and know that I have been chosen to answer a call. I listened with my heart and soul, not my ears and ego. When the messages were complete, I texted my friend to ask if she was ready to hear some messages that I received. She enthusiastically responded by giving me the best phone number to reach her. We chuckled with familiarity as we greeted each other; both of us trusting and knowing the clarity that comes with our special gifts. "I am so pleased it is you," Anne Danielle expressed, as she shared that today was her first day of holidays, and she had asked for someone to speak to her—to guide her. "I received your call then. Are you ready for your messages?" I responded. "Yes, I am ready; let me grab a pen and paper," replied Anne Danielle. With that, I freely unraveled the guidance from her angels, guides, spirits, and ascended loved-ones as clearly, concisely, and comically as they channeled them through me. She was thrilled with new-found clarity and direction for her troubling moments of self- doubt and overwhelming guilt for trying to be everything for everyone all the time. "What divine timing!" we expressed simultaneously. "Now I shall genuinely enjoy my vacation—guilt-free and happy," Anne Danielle said as she thanked me again. I replied with, "My pleasure. I am honored to have been chosen as your messenger today."

The first encounter I experienced with a powerful animal guide certainly challenged my intellect. I was preparing to discontinue a Reiki session with a client who wasn't open to receive. As I was lifting my hands from her feet, I was greeted, in spirit form, by a beautiful, silky, silver-white wolf. Startled at first, I continued to disconnect, when the wolf began to speak to me. His powerful voice and presence mesmerized me, so I paid close attention to his instructions. He insisted that I share his presence, his purpose, and his messages with my client—so I did. I gently touched her arm, as I now stood beside her. I explained that I respect her skepticism and how I was ready to discontinue the session until her guide showed up. Now she became curious and inquired about this guide. I explained to her that this was an unusual guide, and it was the first time for me to experience such a powerful and different guide. I realized, in my hesitation to jump to the revelation, that I was quest-ioning her acceptance of such a bizarre occurrence, especially since she was already so skeptical of the whole situation. At that moment, the powerful wolf guide, in a loud and clear voice, said, "Tell her about me, NOW." So, I did. Her eyes opened wide, and she sat up in amazement. I thought she would certainly run and never return, but no, she was thrilled, and went on to express how she has always had a great love for wolves. She shared how she collects wolf figurines, has wolf wallpaper, wolf blankets, wolf slippers, and other treasures of this wonderful creature that has always captured her attention. Now, more than ever, she was wide open and ready to hear the purposeful and powerful messages that this wonderful animal guide had to share with her. I learned, in that moment, to never doubt what comes through me and to always trust that whatever comes, the client *is* ready to receive. Since then, numerous animal guides have come and have been as profoundly purposeful, effective, and readily accepted.

Other delightful indications of angelic presence that I have experienced include: a gentle knock before Mother Teresa enters the room, brilliant light and warmth whenever Archangel Michael joins in, dancing, flickering lights when numerous angels join in before they fill my head, heart, and soul with their powerful voices and encourage me to share this magical sound through toning, and the delightful swirling colors that entertain me before the angels, spirits, and guides introduce themselves and reveal their names and their purpose.

Know that signs of divine intervention are everywhere, and the more that you open yourself up to their presence, the more you will experience. Be sure not to expect these things; you set yourself up for disappointment when you have expectations. Instead, accept that you are worthy of all great things and that the angels effortlessly appear and speak to you. Always remember to thank them, please.

I encourage you to embrace this magic. Have faith and enjoy!

CHAPTER

Twenty-One

When We Call For Angels
By Thomas Workman

THOMAS WORKMAN

Thomas Workman, Ph.D., is an intuitive channel and angel card reader. He is the co-owner of Camp Joy Ranch (www.campjoyranch.com) with his husband AJ, where they channel a collection of beings they call The Guides, and offer workshops and programs, all to enhance joy in body, mind, and spirit. When not channeling, Tom works for a non-profit social science research organization in the area of health policy. He is the author of numerous academic articles and book chapters, and is delighted to finally focus his writing on his spiritual work.

Acknowledgments

To my husband, AJ, and the amazing group of people who join us for Divine Insights every month, for all their support and encouragement. You are a blessing. To the angels: my deepest gratitude and respect. It is a privilege, honor, and joy to feel your loving presence each and every day. Thank you for keeping me in the divine light. I love you.

When We Call For Angels
By Thomas Workman

For most of my life, I avoided angels. I never thought about them, read about them, or talked about them. I certainly didn't call on them. The truth is, for most of my life, they kind of scared me.

As a kid, angels were merely ornaments. They were characters in a Christmas pageant, and their role wasn't that big: make a few announcements and sing over shepherds in the sky. The entire gig lasted one night. Cartoons would depict angels as someone's conscience, sitting on one shoulder, as the devil sat on the other, trying to talk someone out of eating an extra piece of cake or robbing a store or something like that. I knew it wasn't real—no one had ever whispered in my ear, and even before hitting puberty head-on, I had done plenty of things that someone like an angel should have talked me out of.

Trying to stay on God's right side, I became a bible-carrying, God-fearing, reborn Christian, and since everyone talked about Jesus and ignored angels, I figured leaving them alone was the best course of action. Decades later, I realized the absurdity of trying to be anything other than what I was created to be. Rather than peace, I was filled with frustration and sadness, and by late adulthood, I had reached my breaking point.

I called out for something—anything to change. Within six months, I was moving to a new job, and eventually, an entirely new life. The next three years were filled with new

244

spiritual insights, and the more my mind opened, the more knowledge came flooding in. I could finally question the deep shame I felt about things that had made me who I am, and as I did, these parts of me began to emerge as gifts. I could hear and feel a different sense of the divine that was absent of all pretense. I steered clear of anything religious, including the angels, happy to put newfound faith in the indistinct energies of the universe.

Then all hell broke loose.

Sharp pain in my jaw went from occasional distress to daily and then hourly torture. It kept me from sleeping, eating, or doing anything but rock in agony on my living room couch. No one seemed able to determine its cause, and after extracting a wisdom tooth and the one next to it for good measure, the pain persisted, and in fact, worsened. I took myself off to the emergency room of a large university hospital where they took a scan of my jaw. The result revealed a seething infection that needed immediate surgery. At three o'clock in the morning, they wheeled me into surgery. They woke me an hour later to say they had cleared the infection and I'd be better in a day or two. Within minutes, though, my breathing had become labored. Soon I couldn't sip water without choking, and every breath now crackled like a clogged drainpipe. Less than fifteen minutes after coming out of surgery, I was trying the best way I could to convince the doctors that I couldn't breathe, but they weren't getting it. My last memory was falling backward as the doctor rushed toward the bed.

I don't know what prompted me, but as I was losing consciousness, I called out to archangels Michael and

Raphael. They were the only two angels whose names I knew. I called out their names silently and steadily for what seemed to be an eternity. It was a cry of desperation, and I called out their names in my mind as if challenging these unknown entities to show me the same love I was starting to feel from the heavens.

My first realization as I began to regain consciousness in intensive care, a whole two days later, was that I was still calling out to Michael and Raphael. At first, I wasn't sure if I was alive or dead; unable to open my eyes, I could only hear muffled voices in the distance. If I was alive, then I was in intensive care, and somehow, I already knew that they had performed a tracheotomy to get air back in my body, though, at this moment, I wondered if it had been successful, or done in time. The muffled voices seemed to follow a repeating pattern, and I couldn't feel any pain, or anything at all, for that matter. Maybe I was dead, in some strange transition period before the famous tunnel of light. Or perhaps my old beliefs were right all along, and it was about to go downhill from here.

But I kept calling, even if the archangels might be ignoring me. Their names echoed in the darkness, until I slowly became able to open my eyes to find myself alive. Every possible tube stuck out of me. At the time, I was not sure what I was asking of the angels. Perhaps I wanted them to tell me everything was going to be alright. Not hearing anything, I motioned to a doctor to call my then new boyfriend (now my husband), whom I had fortunately listed as my emergency contact, and tried hard not to cry when he appeared and grabbed my hand, worried the tears alone would drown me.

Over the next few days, as I slowly came out of the fog of the anesthesia, I learned that I had experienced cardiac edema after the surgery, an odd and rare side effect of the blood pressure medicine I was taking. In the first few hours of consciousness, the inability to hear clearly or even open my eyes was because these orifices had closed completely, swollen over by the fluid that turned my head into a basketball. The edema had come on too quickly for the doctor to realize what was happening in time to intubate me, and I had stopped breathing. As if the divine wanted to press the point, there was no one in the gigantic university medical complex with four hospitals and a dental school who knew how to perform an emergency tracheotomy. Eventually, someone punched a hole in my throat to keep me from dying. Apparently, once I was breathing, I was rushed back into surgery to repair my now fractured trachea and correctly fit the breathing tube.

By the third day, the swelling began to recede, and as I woke up, I began to realize the gravity of my situation. My entire breathing and vocal apparatus were diverted, perhaps permanently, and I had a large hole in my throat to breathe from. An active public speaker, much of my career involved my speaking voice, which was now gone. I wondered if any of my life would ever be the same.

If the angels weren't going to show up, I decided that I was going to heal, and knew from past medical challenges that I could create that healing. I was determined to overcome this living nightmare by sheer will. I stayed as positive as possible, smiling and gesturing thanks to every nurse that came in, and doing everything in my power to keep every thought focused on healing, gratitude, and love.

Yet, I would catch myself calling to Michael and Raphael throughout the day, not knowing what I expected of them. A miracle, perhaps? Watching the sunrise from my hospital window after another sleepless night, I repeated their names like a mantra.

Thankfully, my physical healing came relatively rapidly. By the fourth day, the ENT team sent a small camera down my throat and decided to replace my tube with a smaller one. Though harrowing, once the new tube was in, I hoped an end was in sight. On the fifth day, an occupational therapist came to teach me how to swallow water, which was required before the feeding tube was removed. Unable to move from the bed, I happily endured the challenge to get disconnected from the feeding tube and catheter, with the promise of at least a little freedom from my newfound circumstances. Swallowing with a tracheotomy created more of a struggle in courage than I imagined, however, but there was no other way around it, and I eventually got the hang of it. Soon I was up and walking, holding my IV pole and the oxygen tubes that flowed into the angry hole in my throat.

Now transferred to a less intensive care unit, the doctors talked of my eventual release. I held my finger over the tube—a new skill I had acquired—and hoarsely asked when the tube would come out. The nurse smiled, and then handed me a pamphlet on life at home after a tracheotomy, with instructions on the endless care needed to keep myself from infection, occlusion, and a host of other dangers.

For the first time, I gave in to despair. The brave, strong boy who tried to climb each mountain with a smile on his face, fell, deflated and frightened. Looking heavenward, I confessed my resignation: "I can't do this. I've taken every challenge and test you've sent me and somehow got through, but this one has got me. It's too much for me to handle. I'm frightened, and I can't imagine the rest of my life with this reality. I'm done."

Within seconds, a respiratory therapist named Bunny bounced into my room. The look of desperation must have still been screaming from my face, as tears rolled down my cheeks. She took me by both shoulders. "Oh, honey. You got this. You're going to be fine." Her eyes were steady and confident. "Do you trust me?" Such an odd question from a stranger, I thought. But in some way, I knew that she was part of the rescue plan I had somehow been calling for all week. I nodded. She told me she'd be back soon, and that everything was going to be all right.

An hour later, she returned with a makeshift cap for my trach tube. "Your type of trach doesn't have a cap, so I had to innovate something. I'm gonna put this on your tube because I think you're breathing through your nose and mouth. Wanna try?" We both knew in seconds that I was, indeed, breathing without the air tube. "Okay, I'm going to leave this on for the rest of the day. If you have any problems, just pull it off. But you won't. We'll do the same thing tomorrow. After two days, they will close up that hole." Her smile radiated, her eyes sparkled, and I knew she was saying so much more than her words conveyed.

She was teaching me, in an instant, about God's kindness and the truth about angels. They are not mere ornaments or destroyers. They are not our rescue squad either, though they step in as soon as we ask them. Bunny's eyes conveyed a divine secret that has changed my life forever: We share the power of source with the angels, the earth, and each other like siblings share DNA. We are one, and we all, together, create our best outcomes. Bunny's eyes said, simply: You will be fine, for that is the greatest and highest good for all of creation. I had learned that the moment—this moment—is so much more than what you see here and now.

I never saw Bunny again, though someone had told me she had gotten in trouble for what she had done for me. I sense she didn't quite let it bother her. I was home in three days, my tracheotomy removed, my voice thankfully restored, and my life forever changed.

The angels and I often talk now. Images that remind me of their energies surround my home altar, and they've even begun to use me as someone else's "Bunny" when I'm need-ed. Michael's strength is only surpassed by his sense of humor. Metatron's divine geometry is everywhere I look. Raphael's beautiful green glow reminds my heart to smile. Raziel is always encouraging me to use my clairsentience, and stands close every time I read or channel. I am getting to know the others as their energies are called forth by my circumstances. We are a team. They have taught me that together, we and every divine aspect of this living, love-centered universe shines with a single light.

CHAPTER

Twenty-Two

Our Teachers And Our Tools
Ariel, Asrael And Akoya
By Raina Irene

RAINA IRENE

Raina Irene is a heart, soul, and spirit practitioner, and is the owner of Beauty, Strength & Healing, Inc. She is a licensed esthetician, and holds multiple certificates in Holistic Health, Spiritual Work, and Emotional Healing. Raina's eclectic and spiritual diversity enables her to tap into your unique needs, supporting and guiding you to clarity and connecting you with your healing energies. She blends her esthetics with Reiki, crystals, essential oils, and intuition, and holds healing circles with an emphasis on inner wisdom and understanding grief. She educates from a heart of experience. With two siblings, parents, and now a son in spirit, Raina has committed to sharing that our bonds continue. Love is forever—all you have to do is believe and you will see.

Acknowledgments

This story is dedicated to my angels, both in the spirit realm and the earth angels that hold and have held me through the darkest and the lightest experiences on this journey. If your heart said, "She's talking about me," you're right, I am, because you know who you are and I love you. I am so grateful to all of you who support and encourage me to write. Because of my mom and dad, my sister, Sheri, my sons Jeremy, Brian, and Josiah, my daughters Valerie and Aimee, my grandchildren, my most cherished friends, and my husband—the Riches of my life—I continue. I am everything I am because you love me.

Our Teachers And Our Tools
Ariel, Asrael And Akoya
By Raina Irene

Choosing to walk with spirit has not always been easy, but ultimately, it has always been the path I chose. In my youth, I had the privilege of an open dialogue with spirit. My parents never forced me to believe a certain way, although my mother felt a strong tie to her Jewish roots. My father left it up to me to decide, however, he did want me to decide and not flip flop through beliefs that would cause me to be unstable.

My teen years were plagued with familial pain. At age 13, my older sister Joann, who was 15 years my senior, was diagnosed with lupus after her entire body shut down. In the 1970s, doctors didn't know what they know now. Two years after her diagnosis, when I was 15 and she was 30, Joann's body would fail her. My beautiful sister, the one I completely idolized, would leave us. My parents' firstborn, and their only child for a good part of her life, was gone. The unraveling we'd experience in the five years that followed was piercing.

Shortly after Joann left us, my brother Eddie, only two years older than I, crashed his motorcycle and lay unconscious for days. He would wake as "Eddie Two"—his head injury a cross between severe and manageable. He was still reckless, but not completely the same as he once was. Next, my younger sister, Sheri, nine years my junior—I know, quite the family spread—was playing handball in school when she missed the ball and slammed face and fist-first into the wall, breaking both her arms and her teeth. My mother sank deeper into grief, as she now tended to her children who needed her beyond the scope of normal; and my father, a doctor, struggled with despair, wrestling with what he felt was his inability to save Joann and heal Eddie.

At 16, as I was looking in on what my family was going through, I realized that I was facing not only a fork in the road, but the multiple directions each fork could take me. I started down the road of chaos, the inviting one that shows you that you can numb the pain and dry your tears in wild, untouchable colors. That season was short; I was making my mother even more miserable, and if I couldn't touch the colors, how was that going to help me? I wanted more. In fluid movement, the road shifted, and I was introduced to an older woman named Mrs. Elkins. "What a funny name," I thought. In the lifelong clutter of her kitchen, she used an old deck of playing cards to teach me about life, love, and the angels.

One night, as I was lying in bed, I felt a strange energy—paralyzing, yet warm. I heard an audible voice say "I love you," then my body went limp. This happened several times, and while I could not always hear words, I always knew that I had been visited by angels. Once in my early 20s, when I was dating my children's father, I was lying on my bed resting while Mitchell was in the front room. Again, I felt the paralyzing warmth and heard an unknown language. As it faded, my first thought was that Mitchell had come in to say something to me. I jumped off the bed, went into the family room to ask him what he wanted, but then stopped mid-question and instead said, "Oh my gosh, there were two of them!" These light beings, angels, that had been by my bedside, were tall—ten feet or so—light beams of energy that were speaking over me. I continue to be awed and mystified by that evening. Etched in my memory, I can see them right now as if it had recently happened. We would both continue to have visitations from the angelic realm, waking almost nightly at 4:44 a.m., simultaneously hearing what we thought were wings outside our bedroom window.

Angels and spirit continued to guide me as I voyaged forward in my life, but it was the next experience that would set me on *this* tangible walk with the angels. I was doing energy healing on my friend, Becky, and I was standing on her left side when I felt feline energy. "Okay," I thought, "that's interesting." I shared this with Becky as I crossed to her right side, "Becky, there's an angel by your head." I went on to describe this angel, and as I laid my hands on Becky's abdomen, I explained that the angel's message was to, "Have courage." I heard the name Ariel, but I had no idea there was an Archangel Ariel. I was hesitant to say it, since all I could think was, "Crazy girl, Ariel is The Little Mermaid." Doubting myself, and not wanting to be wrong, I told Becky that I heard the name "Airy" or "Airy something." When we were finished, I told Becky to take her time getting up, and then I rushed to the computer to Google Archangel Ariel. To my surprise, there she was, just as I had seen her. As quick as I ran to the computer, I ran back to my healing room. "Becky! Come to the computer! There *is* an Archangel Ariel. Come see!" Becky looked at me and said, "You didn't say Archangel Ariel." Laughing, I told her that when I had heard Ariel, all I could think of was The Little Mermaid. Becky and I looked at the picture in utter amazement. There before us was Ariel with her long braid, a lion—a feline—behind her, and with the word courage across the picture, just as I had described. Both of us gazed at it in astonishment. We unquestionably needed to continue the day together. We both needed to get some shopping done, so we headed out. I was across the store from Becky when I heard her footsteps coming towards me and her eyes were wide with surprise. "Raina!" she exclaimed, "There is a mother over there calling to her daughter. Guess what the daughter's name is? I heard her calling Ariel, Ariel, Ariel." We could not deny it; Archangel Ariel was communicating with us.

And with that, the next fork appeared, the road shifted once again, and I was off to study the angels. Since my encounter with Archangel Ariel, I have gone on to be certified in almost everything angelic. Let me share with you a few of the angels I work with.

Archangel Ariel: Known as the 'lioness of God,' Ariel can help us by providing the means through which we can acquire our physical and material needs. Archangel Ariel is charged with overseeing the natural world. She is closely connected to animals, minerals, and the elemental forces in nature. Ariel is the earth angel; she helps ground us and reminds us to look at all the beauty this earth has to offer. She vibrates to the color of pale pink, rainbow colors, and golden orange. Essential oils that help you connect with her are frankincense, jasmine, neroli, and sandalwood.

Archangel Michael: The name Michael means 'he who is like God.' Known as the angel of strength and protection, Michael comes in severing the chains that keep us weakened.

Archangel Michael is the protector who releases us from fear and doubt. Call on Archangel Michael and you can clear away negative energies surrounding any situation, protecting yourself and everyone involved from negativity of any kind. He vibrates to the color cobalt blue. Essential oils that help you connect with him are frankincense and myrrh.

Archangel Raphael: The name Raphael means 'he who heals,' so you can call on Raphael with any ailment for healing or guidance about the course of action you should take to achieve better health for yourself and others—mind, body, and spirit. If you feel called to be a healer, Raphael can guide you on your journey as well. Raphael vibrates to the color emerald green. Essential oils to connect with him are chamomile, clove, lavender, sandalwood, spearmint, and thyme.

Archangel Gabriel: The name Gabriel means 'messenger of God,' and he is known to help teachers, journalists, and writers communicate effectively. Archangel Gabriel is a powerful and loving messenger of divine love, wisdom, and guidance, and is the archangel of communication, strength, and new beginnings. Gabriel vibrates to the color white. Essential oils to connect with him are cinnamon, clary sage, coriander, melissa, myrrh, neroli, rose, and spearmint.

Archangel Azrael: The name Azrael means 'whom God helps.' Azrael is the angel of transition, and has become my connector since I was introduced to him in a class I took several years ago. Our teacher explained that Archangel Azrael had gotten a bad rap over the years as the death angel—the Grim Reaper—but that's simply not true.

Azrael's main purpose is to help individuals transform from the human life to the spiritual life by guiding them through the translucent doors to eternity. He also surrounds those left behind with divine light and healing energies, helping them cope with the loss and providing spiritual and emotional support. Azrael stands by as a source of quiet strength and comfort. We learned to call in Azrael before connecting to loved ones in spirit, as he is the bridge and protector of the spirit realm. It made sense to me to discover that I have the protection of this angel. I have never had dark spirits around me; they're simply not allowed. But how enhanced would my connection become with the guidance of Azrael? I was about to find out.

My journey would once again be thwarted. This time the earth shift would be more of an underground chute straight to a personal hell. I would need ropes, ladders, spiked shoes, gloves, flashlights, oxygen, a lot of time, love, and without question, the angels to find my way out.

It was a warm California Sunday, October 22, 2017, when I had to make a phone call to a hospital hundreds of miles away. The voice on the other end told me that my son, Josiah, had crashed his motorcycle. They had tried to save him for an hour but—but? I handed the phone to my husband, and the earth opened and swallowed me whole. Complete darkness consumed me. As I cried for my son, I also cried out to the angels, especially Archangel Azrael. "If you are the one that has him, show me where he is and bring him to me. You are the connector." Without ceasing I cried to Azrael, to bring me Josiah. A few years earlier, Josiah had a vision in which he had heard the name "Akoya." He announced to me one day that his spirit/artist name was

Josiah Akoya. Who am I to argue with such a powerful vision? I needed to connect with his spirit. "Azrael, please connect me with *Josiah Akoya,* my *Josiah David*!" Right away, I began to connect, Azrael opened the translucent door, and Josiah showed up, in an alchemy of ways. My cry was and continues to be answered, as I call on Archangel Azrael every day and night without fail. I use cypress, frankincense, cardamom, cedarwood, and sandalwood essential oils on my forehead and my pulse points to open my intuition and create a clear connection. I bathe in his vibration of pale yellow, and ask Azrael to connect me with me to my son, and any other loved ones I may need to bring through.

I am still digging my way out. Each step I take towards the opening gets easier. I don't need any of those tools I once thought I needed to dig with. The light that shines in the darkness is and will always be the love that surrounds us. Love from the angelic realm, our loved ones in spirit, and the love that is right here every day remind me that we are exactly what these angels represent in our lives. They are our teachers and our tools.

We are Ariel's earth angels, charged with overseeing the natural world, and as we do that, it grounds us, so we can see the beauty this world has to offer, which, in turn, fills us with courage.

We have Michael's strength, strong and capable of untangling ourselves from the past, releasing fear and doubt, and moving forward with a new sense of confidence and shelter from the storms.

We are Raphael's healers—the passageway of healing, we are Gabriel's divine love, wisdom, and creativity; and we are Azrael's doorway. We can transform our physical world toward a spiritual life, and see through those translucent doors of possibility, connecting us to infinite love.

As we call on these magnificent angelic beings, they not only help us, they become us.

Side note: That funny last name, Elkins, would become my last name—no relation to my wise kitchen counselor—but the irony that my three children are Elkins is profound, wouldn't you say?

Beauty, strength, & healing, Raina

Final Thoughts From The Publisher

It has been a true honor to work with the authors in this and all our other incredible books. At As You Wish we help authors avoid rejection, your words are our passion.

Visit us at

www.asyouwishpublishing.com

We are always looking for new and seasoned authors to be part of our collaborative books as well as solo books.

If you would like to write your own book please reach out to Kyra Schaefer at kyra@asyouwishpublishing.com

Recently Released

Happy Thoughts Playbook

When I Rise, I Thrive

Healer: 22 Expert Healers Share Their Wisdom To Help You Transform

Life Coach: 22 Expert Coaches Help You Navigate Life Challenges To Achieve Your Goals

Inspirations: 101 Uplifting Stories For Daily Happiness

Upcoming Projects

Holistic: 22 Expert Holistic Pracitioners Help You Heal In A New Way

Manifestations: 101 Uplifting Stories Of Bringing The Imagined Into Reality